THE BUNKER

A TEMPLE BOOK

Atheneum New York 1973

Translated from the French by Esther Malkin
With an Introduction by William Glicksman

BY CHARLES GOLDSTEIN

the bunker

Published by Atheneum
Reprinted by arrangement with
The Jewish Publication Society of America

Originally published in French by Gallimard, 1967
Library of Congress catalog card number 74-116978
Published simultaneously in Canada by McClelland and Stewart Ltd.
Manufactured in the United States of America by
The Murray Printing Company, Forge Village, Massachusetts
First Atheneum Edition

Dedicated
to the sacred memory
of my mother,
who at the age of 77
was tortured to death
during
the deportation to Treblinka;
of my brother,
who was shot
while trying to help her;
and of my sisters and family,
whose time and place of death
remain unknown.

THE BUNKER

introduction

The sufferings and torment of the Jew during the period of the Second World War began the moment he came under German rule. The very presence of a German created an atmosphere of fear and horror; the German became the symbol of death for the Jew. For according to Nazi-German doctrine, the very physical existence of the Jew was illegal. Jews were tolerated only as long as they could do the work of a slave-labor force; their ultimate goal was destruction.

To escape this Draconian existence, many Jews went underground. Some joined the partisan units; some vanished into bunkers. Many died in battle; many hiding places were discovered and their inmates executed.

The Bunker takes the reader into an underground hiding place beneath the ruins of the Warsaw Ghetto. Here a group of seven—six men and one woman—made an attempt to survive in subhuman conditions and in constant fear of being discovered and destroyed.

The narrative begins when the August 1944 Polish uprising against the Germans was coming to an end. Jews who were survivors of the April 1943 Warsaw Ghetto revolt, Jews who came out from their hiding places in and outside the ghetto, Jews who lived illegally as Poles, and many others joined the revolt of the Poles. When the revolt was suppressed, one of the conditions of Polish surrender was the German guarantee that the Polish fighters would be treated as prisoners of war. This privilege, however, was denied the Jews; they were doomed to death.

In August 1944 Charles Goldstein was in a slave-labor unit assigned to clear the debris from the ruined Warsaw Ghetto. The Polish uprising threw him into the whirl of events. He became a soldier in the ranks of the Poles. He fought as a Jew and as a member of human society, motivated by the desire to avenge the death of millions of his people and participate in the struggle against the Nazi-German evil. Because of the conditions of surrender, Goldstein and his companions decided to remain underground. The nightmare struggle for survival lasted from October 1944 until January 1945.

The literature about life in the bunkers and hiding places is, generally speaking, poor. We do not as yet have a sufficient number of accounts of how people lived during those days and nights, weeks, months, and years, some amidst rats and insects, without water or food, and with the only outlet often the city's sewers. Goldstein was probably the first, and certainly one of the first, to describe this underground life. His and his companions' struggle for survival typifies Jewish bunker-resistance against the onslaught of the Germans.

Goldstein's book is neither a novel nor a memoir. It is not the first because it does not contain the fictitious, imaginative elements inherent in a novel; it is not the second because it does not comprise a series of chronological entries. It is rather a witness—a testimony to the suffering of man and to his indomitable fight for dignity and human worth in even the most unbelievably degrading situations. In minute and dramatic detail Goldstein describes how muddy water was madc fit to drink; how soup was made from, almost literally, nothing; he tells of dangerous nighttime forays for food and the agonizing decision of what to do with a dog and its insane master whose presence threatened the discovery of the bunker. While undergoing these experiences, the seven people inside the bunker gave one another strength and made possible their collective will to live.

But Goldstein's account stands out not only because of his description of the physical life in the bunker but also because of its significant presentation of the more intangible elements of man. For ***The Bunker*** is a study of man under virtually unendurable stress, of the conflicts bred by such stress, as well as the loftiest ethical and humane responses conceivable. Much that is ugly and beautiful about man comes to the fore within the pages of Goldstein's book.

There is yet another aspect which did not

escape Goldstein's attention, namely, the relations between Jews and Poles.

Although the attitude of Pole toward Jew had historically been one of hatred and animosity, there had nevertheless always been some individuals and groups who were friendly. This situation changed very little during the war years. With some, the feelings of enmity intensified; with a few, the feelings of compassion grew stronger. This is vividly reflected in Goldstein's narrative.

Just as all through the war years it was often members of the Polish lower classes—peasants, prostitutes, laborers—who concealed Jews for years and thereby helped save Jewish lives, so too in this account it was a Polish worker who risked his life to bring food for the people in the bunker. And it was a Polish priest—an underground fighter—who, having become ill during his concealment in the sewers, was taken into the bunker and cared for by the seven Jews inside until the liberation.

On the other hand, Goldstein did not fail to see the hatred of Poles and the Polish A. K. (Polish underground) unit toward the Jewish combatants on the barricades and upon other occasions. He did not conceal his resentment at such moments; yet he had to overcome his feelings because of the common enemy—the German. For Goldstein, and for many others, the uprising of the Poles against the Germans was a continuation of the Warsaw Ghetto revolt.

The Bunker is an epic which encompasses the depths of human misery and cruelty on the one hand, and the peaks of human endurance and dignity on the other. It is a major contribution to the history of the Holocaust.

William Glicksman

one

"I'm digging a bunker—to bury myself in alive!" Ignace murmurs, as though talking to himself. Tears shine in his eyes and mingle with big drops of sweat which roll down his cheeks. But he goes on digging.

None of the Jews laboring near him respond. Yet they are all thinking the same thing. Still they persist with the digging, putting the last of their strength into it. They are silent, concentrating on one thing alone—to finish digging the bunker as quickly as possible, for they know that for them a moment's delay can mean death.

It is August 1944. The Warsaw uprising, set in motion by the underground Polish Home Army led by Bor-Komorowski, is nearing its end. Warsaw is in ruins. Thousands of dead lie beneath the debris of gutted houses. Many others litter the streets, where fires are raging. The Germans are advancing toward No. 8 Franciszkanska Street, which has been held for many weeks by a Jewish unit.

In these last days of the battle, the Warsaw insurgents have stopped resisting seriously. They know that they are going to surrender to the Germans, that all the combatants will be taken prisoner.

The fate of the Jews is quite different. They are killed on the spot by the Germans. So for the unit fighting on Franciszkanska Street, this bunker is the only remaining chance of salvation.

There are seven altogether. They come from various towns in Poland, France, and Belgium. They belong to different social classes.

Ignace is forty-four. He was born in Warsaw and has always lived there. He used to own a butcher shop in Panska Street. He had had a big family, a wife and six children—all murdered during an "action" in the ghetto. He managed to reach the "Aryan" part of the town, where a Polish woman, a caretaker, hid him in her house until the uprising.

Ezekiel—or as we call him, Haskel—is about fifty years old. He comes from Praga, a suburb of Warsaw. Formerly he owned a little factory where large kettles were made. He and his wife and two children had been hiding in an "Aryan" district of Warsaw. The Germans discovered them and shot his wife and children. Because of his trade, Haskel was spared. The Nazis imprisoned him at Pawiak, where he remained until the uprising.

Isaac is twenty-eight years old, originally from Bialystok. During the occupation, he lived in the ghetto of that town. He managed to escape and to reach Warsaw, where he took refuge in the home of a *Volksdeutsch*—a Pole of German descent. Before the war, Isaac was a medical student. He is married, with one child;

his wife and child were sent to Germany.

Daniel is a youth of eighteen. Originally he lived in Belgium. He was deported with his family. His father, mother, and brother were murdered in Auschwitz. He was taken to Warsaw to help clean up the ghetto. The uprising set him free.

Hannah, twenty years old, is a student from Lodz. She lived in the ghettos of Lodz and Warsaw, then she fled and hid in the "Aryan" district of Warsaw.

Samek, a former chemistry student, is also from Lodz. He, too, experienced the ghettos of his native town and of Warsaw. And like the others, he succeeded later in reaching the non-Jewish part of Warsaw.

I am the seventh. I was deported from France, where I left my wife and two children. At first I was interned in France itself, at Pithiviers; then I was deported to Auschwitz, and from there I was sent to Warsaw to clean up the ghetto—like Daniel. The uprising set me free, and I joined the insurgents to fight against the enemy.

So there are seven of us. Weak, out of breath, sweating profusely, we dig a bunker in the cellar of a half-ruined house which, before the uprising, was No. 8 Franciszkanska Street. This bunker, which opens at one end into the sewer, represents our last hope. We are not at all prepared to live like termites; still, we cling to this idea. We have little to take with us, so very little to eat or drink. But at this moment nothing can deter us. The desire for survival, for escape from the danger which hangs over us, is strongest of all. Despite our clumsiness and inexperience, through our own efforts and the help of some of the Poles, our bunker is at last ready.

The cellar where we have dug our shelter consists of two parts. We leave the first part intact, after having disguised the entrance. In the second, we dig an underground passage six yards long, leading to the sewer—which we prefer to call the canal. We make an opening at the side of the canal so that we can escape if our bunker is discovered. The width of this passage is scarcely half a yard, its height about a yard. As a result, no one can stand up in the passage; one can only sit or lie down there.

At last it is finished. We come out into the yard to look for the last time on the light of day. The sun is shining brilliantly; it is the end of summer. Although our hearts are heavy, the light of the sun and its warmth comfort us and arouse in us some little hope.

The Poles who lived in our house and in the neighboring houses have bundled up a few precious possessions. Clutching these bundles, they are all awaiting the news from the loudspeakers which will announce the end of the uprising, and inform them how they should come out and surrender, and in what direction to walk. A few stray bullets strike the yard; an old man and a sixteen-year-old boy are killed. Were it not for the tears and wailing of the boy's mother, no one would pay any attention, for death and destruction seem the normal thing in this ruined city. Everyone stands or sits as if paralyzed, staring at the wreckage of homes and possessions.

For a long time now, the seven of us have had neither homes nor possessions.Nearly all our families have perished, either in the gas chambers of Auschwitz or in the ghettos. One thought alone occupies our minds. How, once the Germans arrive, can we manage to slip into our bunker?

Fear and hope mingle within us. To bury ourselves in this dark bunker, with little food or water, with scarcely any of the things necessary to man, with no contact whatsoever with the outside world, is to die slowly of hunger and thirst. Yet, at the same time, one spark of hope remains. Who knows? Perhaps we might manage to survive. The Red Army is quite close. Already it is occupying the suburb of Praga; soon, perhaps, before it is too late, it will come and deliver us. We believe it, because even now only the Vistula River separates us from it.

Savage shouting—"All of you, outside!"—abruptly tears us from our thoughts. The Germans are here! Children start to cry and cling more closely to their mothers. They all gather up their parcels and bags, and under the insolent gaze of the conquerors they make their way to the spot to which they are shepherded. Amid the ruins and smoke of the blazing houses, these crushed, exhausted beings, after so many weeks of fighting or of living in the cellars, look like ancient, hollow slaves.

Taking advantage of the panic, we have managed to slip into our cellar, one by one, at short intervals. There we quickly fling ourselves to the ground, hugging the earth as though we want to penetrate it and get as far away as possible from all human sight. Feeble rays of sunshine make their way into the cellar through a tiny grating quite close to the ground. By this fading light, we examine our meager food supply: a paper bag containing a few lumps of sugar, two loaves of bread, and some bottles of water. Muffled noises reach us from the outside. We hear Germans shouting, children sobbing, the noise of stones and bricks falling from demolished houses. These noises are our last links with the outside world, with everything living. Then, slowly, silence sets in as the crying and the sobbing fade away. We realize that our contact with the outside has been cut off; now we are alone. We sense a terrible longing for the outside world. We feel as if we have been buried alive.

Now pale rays of moonlight shine through the grating. Suddenly a loud sound reaches us, like the crackling of a huge, wind-driven fire. The noise gets louder with each passing moment until it suddenly invades our cellar with great force. It is as though a terrible firestorm has broken out above our heads. A red glow shows through the grating, lighting up the cellar for a moment, and then disappears. Smoke begins to pour into our refuge. The ground trembles. Flames are blinding us. The Germans have blown up and set fire to the ruined houses. They are afraid that isolated fighters might still be hiding in half-destroyed building or cellars.

They sprinkle the ruins with gasoline before setting fire to them. Of course they do not overlook No. 8 Franciszkanska Street, neither the house nor its cellar. The building, or what remains of it, catches fire; at this moment our cellar is ablaze and filled with thick smoke.

One by one, as quickly as we can, we slip into the ditch, then crawl toward the opening that leads into the canal; the last one to reach the canal is almost suffocated. We forget we are wading in filthy water, treading on refuse—in places, right up to our knees. We have to get as far away as we can from the fire. Our weariness disappears, but we cannot help trembling.

And yet we have already experienced so many different kinds of anguish: that of the "selections" when a SS murderer, glancing at the rows of deportees, decided by a nod of his head whether or not we were to go to the gas chamber; and that of the "actions" in the ghettos, when our lives depended on almost pure chance and where we could be caught at any moment and sent to a "disposal" center and from there to Treblinka.

Here, in this canal, our anguish is quite different. Thick darkness surrounds us. We cling to each other so as not to be carried away by the current—quite strong at this particular spot. The echo of the water is thunderous in this long, enclosed canal.

To this noise is added the piercing shriek of a whole army of rats, which jump savagely around us. Their hellish noise stupefies us; we think we shall go mad with terror. It is not the fear of dying; no, it is a kind of numb anguish mingled with the regret that our powerlessness causes in us; it is a thousand times worse than being face to face with an armed enemy. It seems that a bottomless gulf has opened beneath our feet, ready to swallow us up at any moment. Transfixed with terror, motionless, not able to retrace our footsteps . . . we wait.

Clouds of smoke continue to invade our bunker. But little by little they thin out and then slowly disperse. With difficulty we retrace our steps, and once again, in single file, we crawl back into the underground passage. There, absolutely exhausted, we sink down onto the ground.

It is impossible to go into the cellar, which is just like a furnace! Besides, the house above, ravaged by fire, could collapse at any moment and entomb us in the debris. So we stay in the underground passage. But even there the heat is infernal. Our wet clothes start to steam; the sickening stench of the sewer continues to pour in through the opening. We are dying of thirst, but we cannot drink yet; we must cherish and guard our sparse supply of water.

Young Daniel lies motionless. He has a temperature, his face is burning, tears roll down his cheeks. From time to time, his lips open in a scarcely audible murmur. As we lie near him, we hear once more the sound of bricks falling outside. It is our house, gutted by the fire, slowly collapsing on top of us.

Big tears pour down Daniel's cheeks. Now and then his hands come together in a gesture of prayer. "Mother, father," he murmurs. Abruptly he jumps up and starts shouting in a strange voice, like a madman: "Father! Father!" He flings himself forward as though wanting to run out. But a deafening noise, like a thunderclap, hurls him back to the ground. We, too, lose our balance and fall down. It is done. Our house has collapsed. Debris rains on our shelter—which manages to resist and remain intact. But the debris covers it entirely; even our grating has disappeared beneath the rubble. We have only one way out: the sewer and its filthy, stinking, noisy waters. We remain silent, rigid, afraid that our slightest movement might unleash an avalanche of bricks and gravel upon us, which would become our tomb. Time passes slowly, heavily.

The half-light and the silence are oppressive. How long should we remain without moving, pressed against the earth in that stifling rabbit hole? Ignace finally decides to do something. He clears a way toward the cellar and goes off to see what has happened. We stay where we are, eyes and ears straining toward the cellar.

Soon we make out a voice choked with tears, a broken voice: "We are lost—there is no way out. We are buried alive; we shall all die here and no one will even know." It is Ignace talking as he makes his way back to us.

At first his despair takes hold of us, too. Each of us envisages his own end—days, weeks, without bread, without water, a gradual loss of strength, a slow, sordid agony among the rats in the canal who watch us, waiting to attack as our flesh weakens, even before death itself.

But the will to live quickly gains the upper hand; one by one we try to reach the cellar to see for ourselves; perhaps we may find a way of getting out. Instinctively we make for the steps by which we came in; but they have disappeared beneath tons of debris. And now each of us longs to do something, if only to make a little hole, a crack, which will look out onto the living world. We forget our weariness, the damp piercing our bodies through our wet clothes, the torrid heat that is making our surroundings like a steam bath. No longer can we think of our empty stomachs or our dry mouths. One overriding desire sustains us: to find a way out, no matter what. We all become human beings again with willpower and energy, and we set to work.

Isaac becomes our guiding spirit. "Don't everybody dig haphazardly," he orders. "Let's go about it methodically. That's the only way to succeed!" Immediately we draw up a plan: to make an opening wide enough for a man to pass through—not in an upright position, but curled up. "It's not so difficult—we'll manage it all right!" These words of Isaac give us back our courage. We set about the task.

We have no tools. Here and there we find bits of wood and we use them like picks. Some of us dig with our hands. For two whole days we go on digging in this manner. We scarcely eat or drink. We must husband our poor reserves as much as possible. With this in mind I propose a sort of "collective bunker diet": three lumps of sugar every three hours and three mouthfuls of water. Four meals a day, as it were. When we are not digging we are sleeping.

On the third day the miracle happens. A tiny chink appears and a narrow ray of light enters the bunker. Cautiously, we widen it. Another moment and we see the sky, a beautiful sky, a splendid sun. The inside of the cellar, though dim, seems to us strangely luminous with sunshine. New hope and courage well up inside us.

two

Suddenly a new danger threatens. Ignace has noticed a huge dog quite close to the house next door. The animal sees him and immediately bounds toward our bunker, barking furiously. Flinging himself back, Ignace hastily blocks up the opening with the help of the stones and bricks that we have piled up there for precisely that purpose. Just in time! The dog has reached the opening and, with his paws, is trying to find a way into the cellar. We all fling ourselves to the ground and crawl toward the canal, our hearts beating wildly. We are sure that the Germans are only a few steps away, in the yard. A dog prowling in the neighborhood certainly must be with someone, and that someone could only be a German.

The minutes go by slowly. We are all thinking of what awaits us the moment the Germans reach our bunker. We are certain that the Germans will not dare to venture into the cellar; they would be obliged to get through a narrow opening one by one, feet first, and we could kill them all.

Instead they will surely use one of two methods they always use when it comes to bunkers: a bomb or gas. In either case, we will die. We console ourselves by thinking: They won't take us alive; they won't be able to humiliate or torture us!

Thus we await our end. At every moment we

seem to hear the noise of footsteps—already our bunker is surrounded, already they are throwing gas or a bomb into it. In this atmosphere of despair, we wait until dark.

Much later, well after nightfall, Hannah gets up and says to us: "I am going out into the yard. Who's coming with me?"

"I'll come!" I tell her, and I start to crawl behind her.

Silently we move away the bricks and stones which conceal the entrance. With great caution we look outside. Brilliant moonlight lights up the ruins; silence reigns everywhere. There is absolutely no sign of any human presence.

We wait another minute, then carefully, slowly, we leave the bunker. This is not an easy thing to do. We bump into a veritable mountain of bricks and stones, and despite our extreme caution—to add to it all, we are barefooted—each of our steps causes a few little stones to fall, and their noise in this deep silence terrifies us. Yet we continue on our way and slowly we approach the half-destroyed house near which the dog was prowling some hours ago.

The house is barely standing, for the fire has reduced the upper stories to ashes. One wall, almost hanging in the air, appears on the point of collapse; it has been burned black. The broken windows, their frames charred, seem like holes in the sky. We come up to one of these windows and look into a room. The moonlight dimly illumines the room, and we see the remains of walls and broken furniture littering the floor. In one corner there is a bed covered with a pile of rags, and close to this bed we see our dog.

Then a head emerges from the rags, and a woman's voice asks in Polish: "Who's there?" The dog begins to bark.

It is impossible for us to take flight: the dog would pursue us. So we reply in Polish: "We're on your side! We're your people!"

Immediately the woman silences the dog. She asks us to come in. The animal seems to welcome us, and when Hannah strokes its head, it lies down at her feet.

The woman pushes aside the rags, and we can see her more clearly. She seems to be over forty. She must have been beautiful at one time, but now she looks almost like a corpse—only her eyes are brilliant and full of life. She has a piercing look which frightens us. "You're Jews!" she says. "You're hiding. I saw you go down in that cellar. You think you can escape, but you'll all die down there."

We do not reply. For a long time an oppressive silence reigns in that half-destroyed room. Then Hannah asks her: "And you? Why have you stayed here in these ruins? If the Germans find you, they'll kill you too."

"It's not the same for me," the woman replies. Her eyes become even more piercing, more brilliant. "I can't go, I have to stay here to look after my children and my old mother. How can I leave them? What would become of them without me?"

She speaks in a serious tone, with conviction in her voice, as if her children and her mother were really there in the other room. But there are no other rooms.

Hannah questions her again. "Where are they, then, your mother and your children? From what I can see, you're all alone."

At these words, the woman jumps out of bed. She takes us by the arm and says in a burning whisper: "Just you come with me. I want to show you."

She drags us toward the window, shows us another ruined house only a few dozen yards away, and begins to speak again, this time in a voice broken with emotion. "I used to live there, with my two children and my mother. Little Felix was twelve, and his sister, Maria, was nine. Casimir, my husband, went off to the war. When he left me, he told me to look after the children, and I did look after them.

"One day I went out early. I wanted to get something for the children to eat; I had nothing left in the house. Our men had already been fighting for weeks; yes, even my little Felix helped them, and he wasn't the only one. Other children, too, would run carrying bottles filled with explosives, to set fire to the German tanks. When I got back with a bit of something to eat, the house was already destroyed. They were all buried under the debris. I couldn't even reach the children or see my mother again."

Her face expresses a deep sorrow, but now there is nothing abnormal in it. Then she changes suddenly, her eyes flame, her voice becomes hoarse as she points her finger at the ruined house. "They're over there, lying in there—and I must look after them. Casimir will be back one day; he'd beat me soundly if he learned I hadn't looked after them, that I'd left them."

We remain rooted to the spot, our throats so tight we cannot say a word. We have forgotten why we left our bunker, where five anguished beings are waiting for us; our eyes remain fixed on the ruins which surround us.

The noise of a brick crumbling to the ground brings us back to reality. We have found neither water nor bread. All we have discovered is yet another danger; this half-mad woman and her dog could bring the Germans down on us.

An idea suddenly occurs to us. It might be best to take the woman with us into our bunker, thus covering our traces. But when Hannah suggests this to her, she quickly jumps back into bed, wraps herself up in her rags, and replies stubbornly: "I can't leave here. How could I? I've got to watch over my children and my mother."

We leave her and go out quietly. The woman silences her dog again. We consider this a good sign. All the same, we don't make straight for the bunker; we go back to it by a roundabout way. We tell ourselves that the woman must not see where the entrance to our shelter lies.

When at last we reach our cellar, our five companions greet us happily and shower us with questions; they are eager to learn what is happening outside. Their good humor vanishes when they learn of the existence of the mad Polish woman. Once again, a deathly silence hangs over our bunker; we are all thinking of this new menace.

It is already very late. We are hungry and thirsty, yet no one dreams of taking a little nourishment or of sleeping. No longer do we see the filthy ground on which we are sitting; nor do we smell the nauseating odor of the sewer, the only air we have to breathe. All our thoughts are concentrated on the woman and her dog. How can we escape this new danger? Have we really any choice?

To tell the truth, there is only one solution. We are all thinking this without putting it into words. All of us are asking ourselves the same question: Is it right that seven people should die because of a single person—or rather because of that person's madness? Nevertheless, we remain silent.

Isaac finally murmurs between his teeth, as if he were talking to himself: "I really am afraid that we shall have to choose between our death and the death of that woman."

Then, again, silence.

Painful moments pass. The will to live struggles with our conscience.

For Hannah and me, this conflict is even more anguishing than for the others. After all, they have not met the unfortunate wretch, so they can imagine her however they like and even see in her an enemy. But Hannah and I can think of her only with pity and compassion. So we propose to our comrades that we wait until the following night; let them, in their turn, go and see her and talk with her. Perhaps they will manage to convince her to join us. In the meantime, we must not remain far from the canal, in order to be ready to fling ourselves into it at the slightest alarm.

They all agree, and I immediately feel that all of them have now relaxed, as though suddenly relieved of a crushing burden. Fortunately, the cruelty and savagery of which we have often been either witnesses or victims have not succeeded in contaminating us. To tell the truth, every one of us prefers to tremble for his life and for that of his companions rather than commit so reprehensible an act.

Calm reigns once more and we decide to rest for a few hours. Dawn is at hand; it is time to sleep after so many harassing days.

We drop off into a deep sleep. How long do we sleep? I do not know. We are awakened by a salvo of gunfire which bursts out quite near us. Immediately, we all make for the canal, certain that the Germans have discovered our hiding place and are after us. But the gunfire stops abruptly.

The rest of the day is quiet. We remain lying down, motionless.

Late in the night, Ignace and Isaac go out into the yard to see if they can discover the cause of the gunfire. Beneath a wall of the half-destroyed house, they come upon the bodies of the mad woman and her dog. The woman must have come out that morning to "see her children" and her dog had followed her; the Germans spotted them and killed them both.

The problem that tortured us the night before is thus resolved in an unforeseen and cruel manner.

Toward dawn we hear sustained cannon fire which appears to come from quite close. It shakes our bunker and seems to be directed against Praga, from which an immediate counterfire breaks out in reply. Shells fall near our bunker. No possible doubt of the fact—we are caught between two fires.

The artillery duel between the Russian and German armies makes our situation very precarious. At any moment a shell could hit our bunker; then German sentries could quite easily spot us.

But the most serious problem is that of food. How is it possible to get any in such conditions? Haskel, our "forager," is more and more gloomy. He mutters between his teeth: "Soon we'll have had our last mouthful of water; soon there'll be no more sugar." No one answers him.

We are all lying near the outlet to the canal, ready to take refuge in it at the least alarm. Then it is night once more. The artillery duel becomes sporadic, until finally it ceases completely.

None of us says a word, but we are all brooding over the same question: How can we get hold of something to eat and drink?

We see Isaac get up. The noise of an iron utensil reaches our ears. Armed with an improvised bucket, Isaac is making his way toward the canal.

"What are you trailing that bucket down there for?" Ignace asks him.

"I want to get us some drinking water."

"You're mad!" Samek exclaims. "That filthy water's full of rats. Is that what you want to drink?"

Isaac does not answer him. He goes down to the canal and is soon back. With great care he holds his bucket in both hands so as not to lose a drop of the precious liquid and calls my name. He holds out the bucket to me and as quickly as possible starts crawling toward the bunker. When, breathless, he finally reappears among us, he gleefully rubs his hands together and says to me: "We'll have water; we don't need to worry about that."

Nobody answers him; we are all thinking he is losing his mind.

Isaac smiles at us. "You think I'm crazy? Well, you are wrong. We'll filter this water and we can drink it quite safely. I know what I'm talking about—I was a medical student. We've got a bit of coal here, and we can get a bit more. At night we'll go out in the yard and get wood; we should easily find some among all the debris. We'll make a fire, and we'll have boiled water."

At first we are all stupefied. Then Samek exclaims: "An excellent idea! I'll go with you. During the uprising, people lived in cellars and took whole piles of things down into them. Even the fires can't have reduced everything to ashes. We'll find plenty of things that will be useful for us, and even some food."

Young Daniel, still weak, gets up; he too is very enthusiastic. "Do you think I'm going to stay here? I'm coming with you. During the rebellion, we made underground paths so we could pass from one yard to another. We pierced holes in the walls so we could keep in contact with our neighbors. I used to take arms to the insurgents through these underground passages; more than once we passed messages through those cracks in the walls. We can use the same paths. I know them well—I can guide you!"

Our young, delicate Hannah says with her shy smile: "Well, I'll stay here and tidy up the place. If you do find anything to eat, I'll be able to cook it for you. To tell you the truth, I've never done any cooking, but I'll learn."

We are all smiling now; the atmosphere is relaxed.

While waiting impatiently for nightfall, we draw up the rules of our Bunker Group:

(1)During the day absolute quiet must be maintained; no one is to move; silence is to be kept so that no sound will betray our presence. For the Bunker Group, "day" begins at nightfall.

(2)Those comrades whose responsibility it is to

obtain supplies for the bunker must bring everything they find into the cellar. Under no circumstances may anything they come across be kept for themselves; everything belongs to the group and must be put at the disposal of all the members of the group.

(3) If one of us falls into the hands of the Germans, he must on no account, even under torture, reveal the whereabouts of our bunker. That is a sacred oath which each of us must maintain whatever the cost.

These short rules will help us later to overcome the most difficult moments, for each of us will know that he is no longer alone, but bound to his companions. Our jobs, and our attachment to each other, will make our withdrawal from the world much easier.

At nightfall Isaac is the first to rise. "Come on. Let's be off now!"

Samek and young Daniel get up immediately and crawl toward the exit. They are all barefooted so that their footsteps will not be heard. When they have gone, Ignace stays a bit longer near the opening, his ear to the wall to make sure that nothing is moving in the yard. Then we wait.

Some minutes pass. A burst of gunfire breaks

the silence and soon, like an echo, another burst replies to it. This is repeated five times in succession. We are transfixed with fear. Hannah weeps quietly in her corner. Haskel, as is his habit, mutters a few words. "It's with such bursts of fire that my wife and children were killed." Ignace, lying face down near the exit of the bunker, does not even dare to raise his head. As for me, I want to say something but no words will come. I slip down beside Ignace and look outside.

Time seems to stretch out endlessly. The ruins around us give off a kind of terror. This is all that remains of what was once Warsaw. On this very spot Jewish life went on at its fullest. Down there, a little further on, is Muranowski Square. I lived there in days gone by; I worked there; it was there I struggled for existence like so many other Jews. . . . There is my house and my secret meeting place with friends. . . . My departure for France, then Auschwitz, and later my return to Warsaw with a platoon of prisoners. . . .

The sound of bricks falling to the ground drags me back from my reflections. I can make out Isaac and Samek. They are approaching the bunker from two opposite sides. They are scaling piles of stones. Both of them are carrying parcels. Another moment and they are once more among us.

"Where's Daniel?" we all exclaim at once.

"We have no idea," Isaac replies. "As soon as we heard the firing we raced into a cellar for cover, and then into another one. Then we realized Daniel wasn't with us."

No one even glances at the parcels Samek and Isaac have just brought, and our "provisioners" do not say a word. Haskel murmurs between his teeth: "He is little more than a child; we shouldn't have allowed him. . . ." Each of us goes in turn to the bunker opening in the hope of seeing Daniel, of hearing the sound of his footsteps again.

Then Ignace hurriedly comes down from the pile of stones that serves as our observation post. "He is coming, there he is!"

A moment later young Daniel is among us. Under his arm he is carrying a little parcel, which he places on the ground with great care; then he sits down, out of breath. We wait for him to get his breath back. Then he tells us what happened.

"When I was close to the first cellar, I bumped into a pile of bricks, which began to crumble beneath my feet. A second later, I heard gunfire. I went down into the first cellar I came to and there I lay, listening intently. I thought it was a German patrol alerted by the noise of those stones, and any second I expected soldiers to arrive. But it wasn't that at all, because the gunfire became fainter and fainter. Then I thought the sentry near our bunker might have fired to alert other sentries. I waited there a long time; then I went into another cellar, then into a third, and it was there that I found this lamp. Now we shall be able to have some light."

"Well, we found some rice, oats, and also something to make a fire with," Isaac declares gaily. "Now we only need to filter the water."

Samek takes hold of the lamp, examines it with great care as one would a very precious, costly object, then announces: "It's still in good working order. That's a good omen. We have found light."

Haskel sets up our stove: he puts one brick next to another, and over these he places two bits of iron which will serve as a support for the saucepan. He sets up this cooker quite near the exit opening onto the canal, so that the smoke can escape. Hannah and Isaac filter the water, then they prepare the rice.

A little while later we enjoy a hot meal. Ignace gaily teases Isaac for not having been able to get some salt. "How can you have a housewarming without salt? It's a Jewish custom to bring some salt to a new home." We all laugh.

With daybreak, the artillery starts again. It reminds us that for the seven in the bunker "night" is beginning. Although we are concerned about the possibility of German patrols coming back during the day to continue searching through the ruins, we blow out our lamp and lie down happy—for the first time in many weeks.

three

The sufferings we had experienced before our life in the bunker, the atrocious conditions in camps and ghettos, taught us that man is capable of bearing even that which might seem at first to be beyond human endurance. Our existence in the bunker now provides us with yet another proof of this. After some days spent underground, the endless artillery fire above our heads, as well as the nearby explosions, no longer seem to disturb us. We have grown accustomed to them, just as we have to the hard, damp earth of our cellar. In the beginning, when artillery shells or bombs dropped from aircraft fell a few yards from our shelter, it seemed that, like the ravaged earth itself, we too would be blasted into the air. But now, seeing that this has not happened, we merely press ourselves a little closer to the earth, barely feeling its hardness. Soon we are asleep once more.

It is another matter altogether when we hear the sounds of human beings. Not even the faintest noise from the yard escapes us. We remain alert even in sleep. There is nothing astonishing in that: to be discovered is our greatest fear. That is why, like watchdogs, we strain to catch every sound; for us, footsteps are an alarm.

Such an alarm occurs the day after our foraging expedition. Hannah is the first to realize the danger. Immediately she murmurs into Samek's ear, he being closest to her: "Someone is walking around behind the wall!"

She has hardly finished this short sentence when we all hear, very clearly, the noise of approaching footsteps. At first it seems the sound is coming from the cellar opposite our bunker. But a few seconds later we realize that someone is walking about in the cellar beneath the neighboring yard. Besides the noise of footsteps, there are the sounds of things being flung to the ground, moved or pushed from one spot to another, as well as the noise of a very loud conversation. Although the meaning of the words escapes us, we can hear well enough to realize that the language being spoken is German. The German patrol of last night must have reported suspicious noises in the yard, and now Nazi soldiers are hunting for men hidden underground. When they finish searching the cellar next door, they will reach ours.

At that moment I am sure we can all foresee our bunker wall collapsing beneath Nazi axes, and soldiers falling on us like wild beasts. There they are—showing their teeth in a broad smile. What a catch! Seven Jews at once!

Normally in such a situation you look frantically for a way out. But sometimes the threat of mortal danger paralyzes the victim's brain, and this is what happens to us at this moment. Without moving, we remain near the canal opening

—without even trying to take refuge there! I feel myself succumbing to a paralyzing indifference. My will to live becomes weaker and weaker, and I seem to hear deep down inside me a voice repeating: "I've suffered enough! Death is preferable to this kind of life!"

But suddenly I see the SS at work in full fury —as I have seen them so many times in the ghettos and concentration camps. I imagine the SS commandant directing the search around the bunker and finally reaching us. I see his sadistic smile. I can almost hear the coarse laughter of his soldiers. The indifference within me gives way to anger.

"Why are we staying here?" I murmur impatiently. "What are we waiting for?" Without waiting for anyone to reply, I crawl toward the canal. The others begin to get up and follow. Only Samek remains in the passage, straining his ears toward the bunker to hear what is happening outside.

The noise grows louder. Reinforcements have arrived. Suddenly we hear a cry of triumph, accompanied by breaking glass. It is not difficult to guess that the soldiers have found cases of wine or brandy in the neighboring cellar. They start drinking. Soon they have forgotten the purpose of their search. It seems to us that other groups too have come to take part in the festivities. The drinking goes on.

At last we hear the sound of a car, and bottles knocking against each other. The soldiers are stocking up. The car goes off. Silence descends once more.

Quietly we make our way back to our bunker. We sink to the ground, half dead, and remain very still for quite awhile, each of us battling for control of his nerves. As always after such an alarm—and there are to be many of them—we are drained of strength, more worn out than after the most laborious work.

Slowly we grow calm. Young Daniel breaks the silence. He speaks softly, as though to himself. "I've lived a long time with death in the camps. We were always on the alert. The slightest distraction, the slightest relaxation, could cost us our lives. But my nerves were never so much on edge as they are in this miserable bunker. You can go mad here!" He shouts rather than speaks these last words, and all of a sudden he bursts out sobbing.

"Yes," Ignace says. "You really can."

"We didn't realize what it means—a bunker!" Samek adds quietly.

"We mustn't allow our spirits to sink like this," Hannah interrupts severely. "If we don't watch ourselves, we won't be able to hold out for long."

"Hannah is right," I say. Then I add: "It is more difficult to live in a bunker than in a ghetto or a camp, where at least you're in contact with the world of the living."

"A pretty 'world of the living' Auschwitz is," Haskell says, his words as clipped as his manner. "Go on! That was a world in which every one of us was simply waiting his turn to be slaughtered."

"All right," I reply. "A world of the dead. But at least there was a certain freedom of movement and you could see the world of the living through the barbed wire—so close you could almost touch it, feel it, join up with it even if only through the strength of your thoughts. There you could only think of one thing: what you could do to endure until the moment when you'd be able to get back to that free world. Here we are cut off from the outside world. We lie in this black bunker, and we imagine the outside world by picturing the ruins of Warsaw. You could indeed go mad if—"

"Well, then, what do you think we should do? Isaac asks, a trace of anger in his voice. "Perhaps you will be kind enough to tell us, you who know everything!"

"You shouldn't get angry, Isaac," Hannah remarks. "Everyone's entitled to say what he thinks."

"What should we do? We should cling with all our might to the world that exists outside this bunker, beyond the ruins of Warsaw. We should tell ourselves continually that farther off there exists a world where we should like to live. If we believe that sincerely, we shall be able to overcome our weakness."

For a long moment no one replies. Then Hannah sighs deeply. "What you say is very reasonable. But it's so hard!"

How much like children adults sometimes are! A piece of candy from its mother quickly soothes away a child's tears. So it is with us. A few words are sufficient to alter our state of mind completely. We are hopeful once more.

We remain that night in the bunker and do not light our lamp, in case the Germans have left guards in the vicinity. After a brief discussion, we decide to remain in our hole for several nights on end, in order to persuade the Germans of the futility of their searching. We still have some oats, although we think it would be better that night to do without a hot meal. Our decisions serve to calm us down.

One of our companions, Haskel, worries us. He is taciturn. On the rare occasions when he speaks, it is only to mutter a few words which are not in the least comforting. He frightens us. Who knows? Perhaps he carries inside him some terrible memory. We often talk of it among ourselves. On several occasions we have asked him to tell us his troubles. Once Isaac even pretended to be angry: "Why do you never say anything? You insist on keeping silent and all you do is mutter in corners." It was a waste of time. We've already given up trying to make him talk. We decide not to send Haskel out on his own in search of food, for he might never return to the bunker.

After the experience with the German patrols, we do not move from our bunker for three days—they feel like three years! By the fourth day our reserves of food are exhausted, and we decide to resume our explorations. Lying in the semidarkness, we wait impatiently for the right moment. All of us are eager to get out of the bunker, if only to go into the nearest cellars—which in itself is an extremely dangerous undertaking, for we could run into a German patrol and be shot. In spite of this, nobody hesitates. First of all, the more foragers there are, the richer our booty will be—a useful precaution, especially in case of any unforeseen event which could prevent us from leaving our bunker again. And besides, our nerves are on edge, and an hour's escape seems desirable, even in the face of great danger.

The previous night Haskel seemed calm and relaxed; without asking anyone, he began to construct a separate area in which we could relieve ourselves. With a few old rags, he made a curtain with which he screened off a corner of our bunker; then he took a plank which had a hole cut in it and set it on an old cooking pot, which was thus transformed into a kind of lavatory basin. That was a very useful thing, for before that we had all been forced to crawl away with great difficulty, then bend right over the canal.

When he was done, Haskel even risked making a little joke. "And now," he said, "we have a dwelling with all the modern conveniences." Then, toward daybreak, he lay down to sleep, as did everyone else.

Now a heartrending cry wakes us up. "Shoot me at the same time as them! Shoot me too!" In the darkness we make out a shape running toward the exit and stripping off its clothes. It is Haskel. Quickly we reach him and pull him back. He resists like a lunatic, all the while shouting and screaming.

Isaac slaps his face, hard.

Immediately, Haskel calms down. We take him back to his place. For a long time afterward we hear him weeping softly and murmuring: "Why should I still be living?"

four

That night four of us go out foraging: Ignace, Isaac, Daniel, and I. We split up into two groups. Ignace and Isaac go off in one direction, Daniel and I in another.

The first few steps are always the most terrifying: we have to climb the mountain of bricks and stones which covers our bunker. At each step, debris rolls down with a noise which, in the silence of the night, seems to us more terrible than it probably really is, and we fear that the sound of our footsteps might reach the ears of the German sentries who are still keeping watch almost everywhere in the destroyed city. It is only when we succeed in slipping into a cellar that we breath more freely.

Indeed, in the cellars we feel safe. The cellars are our friends, and we think it unlikely that we will encounter Germans there. All we see there are rats, busy around the corpses that seem to eye us from beneath the piles of wreckage. In fact, the danger inside these cellars is considerable—going from one to another, one could very easily fall into the arms of the angel of death. But our need to obtain something to eat is so imperative that we become indifferent to peril.

Our underground expeditions develop a pattern. All of us have matches and candles. At the very beginning of our stay in the bunker, we found a packet of candles. So before even going into a basement one of us lights a match to see if the room contains anything at all or if it is entirely empty, if it is intact or ravaged by fire. If we see that the room contains something, one of us lights his candle, all the while shielding it carefully with his hand so that the flame is not visible through the grating, while the other gathers up everything which might be useful to us. In the case of the cellar's being empty or destroyed, we make our way into the next one.

Tonight we are lucky; in the first cellar we find a treasure—salt! It is not real salt, but grains of dried-up salt mixed with fish scales; we find this at the bottom of a herring barrel. But it is a magnificent find. Both of us are so overjoyed we exclaim in unison: "Salt!" and our faces glow with happiness. Unable to say a word more, we look at each other and embrace, then we taste this precious salt—a real delicacy!

We inspect the cellar and notice that it has no opening at all. We find no trace of human presence, nothing to indicate that men had hidden here during the uprising. On the contrary, one thing strikes us immediately: one of the walls of the cellar is almost entirely covered by coal carefully piled up right to the ceiling. We examine this coal closely and reach the conclusion that it has been piled up here for some specific reason, probably to disguise an entrance to a second cellar, where there might be food supplies. After moving aside part of the coal, we do indeed discover a hole in the wall which seems to confirm the existence of a second cellar. Daniel lies down full length on the ground and, covering a candle with his hand, peeps through the crack. Then he leaps up hastily and draws back, stifling a cry.

"What's the matter? What did you see?" I say in his ear. But he cannot utter a word. Finally he points toward the second cellar and whispers: "Dead Jews!"

Immediately we move aside the rest of the coal piled up at the entrance and make our way into this second cellar. What a horrifying sight! The remains of human bodies lie on the ground —arms, legs, half-eaten by rats and covered here and there with scraps of typically Jewish clothing, such as pious Jews in our country used to wear.

We remain where we are as though petrified. I feel faint. Daniel trembles. Without a word we take two pieces of wood and cover the remains of the bodies with earth. When we are done, we slip outside. Only then do we realize how much time has elapsed. No question of exploring other cellars now! We must be satisfied with the salt we have found in the herring barrel.

Dejected, exhausted, we reach our bunker. There we find Isaac and Ignace. They have unearthed precious objects: a bag containing a few pounds of flour, a small quantity of barley, and some beans. We sit around the fire on which the barley is boiling, its odor delicately teasing our nostrils. All is ready; they were only waiting for us to return.

Hannah sets the table. It is quite idyllic. My glance meets Daniel's—we understand each other without words; no, we must not tell our friends what we found in that neighboring cellar, not now.

We show them the salt. Our companions' joy knows no bounds.

Samek whistles his admiration. "Oh ho! Lunch is no better than this even at the Bristol!"

"The Bristol?" Ignace says. "I've never eaten there, never set foot in the place. But I know one thing: whatever the menu of the Bristol offers its customers, they will certainly not enjoy it half as much as we shall our barley."

And so dinner passes in an entirely gay atmosphere. There is much joking. Ignace pretends, seriously, to have found a bone in his "dish." Isaac assures us that it is not barley we are eating but a pudding for the Sabbath prepared exactly according to his mother's recipe. I glance around the "table" where we are all seated and at our "apartment"—this sordid bunker, with its noisome ground and sinister shadows thrown by the feeble light given off by our poor lamp in the corner. From the nearby canal come the festering odors of the sewer. I think of the extraordinary power of the will to live. The slightest pleasure wipes out all our ills. We can even be gay. Hope is reborn. Better still, old habits from our free life of former days begin to return.

Young Daniel seems quite joyful and looks at Hannah with eyes so full of love that you feel he will immediately begin whispering a thousand sweet words in her ear, as if they were sitting alone in a beautiful garden in the moonlight. But when Samek comes up to Hannah and puts his hand on her shoulder, Daniel's face changes. He betrays the sudden, sad shock that Samek's gesture has aroused in him. Yes, life with all its complications, all its old habits, begins to penetrate our bunker.

That Hannah and Samek are in love was obvious to all of us from the very start of our communal life.This love dates back to the days before the bunker; down here it has only grown stronger. But it has also come to our notice during the last few days that Daniel loves Hannah too. Hannah's continuous presence—pretty, lively, scarcely twenty—has awakened in him feelings which were slumbering in his heart; and now our eighteen-year-old Daniel often lies down for hours, speaking to no one, looking at the ceiling. All kinds of thoughts must be going through his mind: his own sufferings, the tragic death of his parents, the nostalgia for family and home, and also that desire, still vague, which certainly he himself could not have defined. Often he leaves the bunker, slips down to the canal, and walks about there for hours on end, listening to the noise of his own footsteps.

To tell the truth, to go for a walk in the canal has become a habit very precious to all of us. It is our favorite pastime, the best means we have of distracting ourselves a little and of calming our nerves. There is nothing surprising in that. Life in the bunker is monotonous. With nightfall, "day" begins for us, and we prepare ourselves for our foraging expedition. Usually four of us go out, and Hannah and two others stay in the bunker to prepare the meal and to filter the water. At about two o'clock in the morning, unless something unforeseen arises, the "explorers" come back and we sit down at the table. Those who have been out relate what is happening outside, what they have seen in the yard, what the newly explored cellars revealed, and so on.

Each cellar has its "personality," its own story, which shows us to what kind of people it belonged. We judge the cellars, first of all, by the food and clothing we find there; these reveal the social level of the owners. Certain cellars are completely destroyed, either by bombs or by fire; they bear witness to past battles, to a persistent resistance on the part of their occupants, to the heroism of hounded men forced into slavery who, nevertheless, did not become degraded by it. As time goes by, we are forced to go farther away from our bunker, for the number of cellars which have been destroyed is very great and even those which have remained intact are often completely empty. We mark with a special sign the cellars we have already searched, so as to avoid wasting our time searching them again and also to make it easier for us to find our way back. All the same, it often happens that we are forced to go down into one of our previously explored underground retreats, especially when a sound from somewhere seems suspicious to us and we think it prudent to hide. Sometimes, too, after having made a false step, mounds of debris crumble beneath our feet and force us down into the first cellar we can reach. After such expeditions, we feel the sharpest longing for a normal walk free from fear, and this is only possible in the canal.

Each day—that is to say, each night—one of us escapes from the bunker to go for a walk there. The canal network follows the design of the streets above it. Thus the principal canal corresponds to the main highway above it; the smallest canals and the very tiniest ones are situated directly beneath the little streets and alleys. The principal canal is broad and high, and we can walk comfortably there, even if there are several of us together. The little canals are narrow and low; we cannot stand up in them and in certain places it is even impossible to sit down. All these little canals empty into the big one, and it, in turn, pours its waters into the Vistula.

In this network of canals we discover crossroads; the canals which meet there form a kind of square, just as the streets above them do. After the insurrection and the deportation of almost the entire population of Warsaw, the inflow of water and refuse into the canal decreased with each succeeding day; it became increasingly easy to find completely dry areas.

One evening Haskel goes for a walk in the canal—to "take the air," as we laughingly say. An hour or two go by. Suddenly we hear him running toward the bunker with such haste that we immediately think that the Germans are on his heels. We are thunderstruck, for in case of an attack from the direction of the canal we are lost. We have nowhere else to take refuge. Soon Haskel is among us, out of breath, shouting: "Water! Water!" At first we think he is ill and asking for a drink; but he pushes away the container we give him. "No, I've just discovered—I've found water, real water, pure, a spring."

We look at each other and think that Haskel

has lost his mind. How is that possible? A spring of pure water in this stinking canal? But Haskel, who meanwhile has managed to get his breath back, relates what he has discovered.

He had gone for a walk as usual, moving with one hand against the wall. Suddenly his hand encountered space—no more wall! He stopped, struck a match, and realized that he was on a little square, unwalled, where several canals met. He noticed that part of this square was dried up. Suddenly, he heard the noise of water falling drop by drop. He went on a few steps, struck another match—his last one—and there he saw, filtering through a wall, a spring of pure water. He couldn't believe his eyes. He stayed on that spot, motionless, without taking his eyes off the spring, straining his ears for the noise of the falling drops. Then he went closer and let a few drops fall on his hand. No doubt about it! Pure water!

"Come with me and you'll see for yourselves."

Everyone wants to go with Haskel but someone has to stay in the bunker; at last, three of us follow him, Isaac, Daniel, and I.

Haskel goes first; the rest of us bring up the rear. Isaac is convinced that the story has no foundation, that it is purely and simply the result of Haskel's sick imagination. What is more, he is still annoyed with Haskel because of his headlong rush back into the bunker which terrified all of us.

We walk along quickly and soon reach the spot. Isaac lights a candle, puts it near the place Haskel has indicated, and we all see the drops of pure water falling one by one from a little hole channeled in the wall.

The drops are no larger than the tears of joy which fill our eyes. But what does that matter? This tiny spring becomes, in our minds, a veritable well; we shall fill buckets and buckets from it endlessly, and we shall be able to quench our thirst with pure fresh water, without being forced to rely upon the dirty water from the canal.

For quite a time we stare in silent wonderment. Then Isaac leans forward and makes a little cavity in the ground, so that the water can gather together in a single place. We watch how, drop by drop, the water forms a tiny, limpid pool. We are overwhelmed with joy!

The first to come back to reality is Daniel. He returns to the bunker to bring the pot and the bucket. Hannah, Ignace, and Samek come back with him. They, too, want to see the miracle.

Daniel has brought a bit of sand. He spreads it out on the muddy earth surrounding the spring. Patiently, we wait until the water accumulates; the sound of these drops is for us the most beautiful music in the world. When the first pot is full, each of us tastes the water; it is like nectar, the taste of life. We now have pure water to drink and use for cooking.

Finally, we start back to the bunker. Haskel does not come with us. He wants to remain a little longer near his spring. Daniel decides to stay with him.

The rest of us are making our way slowly back to the bunker when we hear the noise of a cough coming from the canal. Isaac quickly puts out his candle. We stop, hold our breath, and listen. Silence. But all of us heard the cough. Carefully, we skirt the canal wall and crawl through the opening into the bunker. We lie down, each in his corner. For a long time we stay like this, in total silence. Suddenly we hear a noise from the direction of the canal: the footsteps of Daniel and Haskel. As soon as they see us, they signal to us not to speak. In one hand Haskel is holding the bucket, which is almost empty; with the other he helps himself to climb in. Daniel, who follows him, is extremely pale. Quietly he tells us they heard someone coughing in the canal and the sound of an object thrown into the water. They blew out the candle and returned immediately to the bunker.

No one says a word, no one asks any questions. Our new situation is clear. All our calculations, all our projects, are reduced to nothing. Until that moment, we thought that the threat could only come from outside, from the bunker entrance, and we considered the canal as an absolutely safe place, a refuge in case our bunker was discovered. Now it is obvious that the danger is coming precisely from the canal itself—an even more terrible menace, since we can do nothing against it.

The fact that the danger is so close and at the same time so mysterious frightens us almost beyond endurance. How the atmosphere has changed since barely two hours ago! At the discovery of the spring we were so gay. Now we are in despair. Everything is black, menacing, with no way out. We are crushed by this violent and rapid change. We feel lost, and lie on the ground completely helpless. In our confusion, we even forget to post someone near the opening to the canal to keep guard.

Artillery fire drags us from our apathy; for us this is the signal that our "day" has ended and our "night" has begun. Isaac takes up his position near the opening onto the canal. But no one can sleep. We lie with our eyes wide open. From time to time we glance anxiously toward the canal. The slightest noise terrifies us. Over and over again, it seems to us that someone is coming toward our shelter. We tell ourselves that we have no right to wallow in this despair; we must defend ourselves; we must do something. But what? Nobody knows.

The artillery fire continues and increases in ferocity. Cannons thunder with violent force. Haskel murmurs between his teeth, in a strange voice that we scarcely recognize: "Let it finish; I can't go on anymore! Let a shell fall on the bunker and bury us all forever. I've had enough, enough!"

A shell explodes near our bunker and interrupts Haskel's murmurings. The shell has fallen so close that all around us the earth trembles.

Isaac comes back from his position near the entrance to the canal, and tells us in a low voice: "I've heard suspicious noises again, coming from the canal." We are silent once more; then, still silent, we begin to move one by one toward the underground passage. There we wait, prepared to fight.

Hannah murmurs, as though talking to herself: "We could be mistaken. Perhaps they aren't Germans, but fugitives like us hiding in a bunker that opens onto the canal."

We are quick to agree, clinging with wild hope to Hannah's suggestion. Perhaps they are fugitives. Who knows, maybe they are as much afraid of us as we are of them. They might be members of the Polish Resistance who have chosen to live underground rather than be captured by the Germans. They might even be Jews. These thoughts fill our minds until nightfall, when the artillery stops.

We find we can bear the uncertainty no longer; we must find out who is down there on the other side of the canal, otherwise we shall be condemned to tremble at the least noise and to give up our precious find—the spring. So we decide to put off our usual foraging expedition to the following night. Instead of searching the neighboring ruins for food, we propose to find out who is on the other side of the canal.

Three of us take part in this excursion, Isaac, Daniel, and I. Isaac goes first, carrying a candle. Daniel and I follow. Our footsteps echo in the canal. We make our way toward the spot the coughing came from the night before. When we think we are there, we stop, and Isaac shouts in Polish: "Who's there?"

We wait a moment, tense, scarcely breathing, straining our ears. Nobody answers. After some minutes, Isaac shouts again: "Answer us! We are Jews!"

Once again—silence. But soon we hear footsteps and see a light. It seems to come from a lateral canal; it is coming nearer. Because of the darkness, we cannot see who is carrying the light. A voice replies in Polish: "We are your comrades!"

We come nearer still, and before us we see a fairly elderly man with a tired, emaciated face. For a moment we look at him, incapable of saying anything at all. He smiles at us; we smile back. That is how we say hello to each other. But soon our ability to speak returns. The man says to us: "My name is Joseph. I live here with my three comrades. We are Poles. Come with me. I'll show you our hiding place. It is close by."

After walking only a minute or two, we reach the spot where the canals cross. Joseph leads us toward the corner of a lateral canal and announces in a loud voice: "This is where we live, and here are my comrades." We greet each other warmly and embrace. Automatically we feel a kinship with these men, and we notice that their attitude to us is warm and friendly. There is not the slightest barrier between us. Here we are not Jews and Christians; we are all persecuted by the same enemy. All of us belong to the same world, an underground world unknown to human beings and appreciated only by the rats who run here and there, squeaking shrilly.

We look at their living quarters and are especially impressed by the planks which they have turned into bunk beds. Joseph notices this and gives us some details.

"All this was prepared before the end of the uprising. We had fought from the beginning in the Old Town, and we were the first to drive out the Germans. During the insurrection, we had to use the canal as a refuge on more than one occasion. And when the insurrection was nearing its end, we decided to come down here; we could no longer bear the sight of the Nazis. During the last two days of the uprising, we prepared these planks and collected some provisions. Almost at the very last moment, we came down into the canal through an opening which is a bit farther up and we managed to drag ourselves right up here."

Joseph stops to get his breath back, then he goes on. "At the beginning it was very hard. Everything was flooded by the canal waters, which came right up to our plank beds. It was impossible for us to walk one step and keep our feet dry. Only by remaining sitting or lying on our planks could we avoid contact with the water. Today, the situation is incomparably better. It is dry almost everywhere. But we cannot hold out any longer. Our food supply is exhausted; we have scarcely any drinking water left. The dampness from the canal penetrates our bones. Kazik here is already coughing. Look at him. If he stays here, he'll only make a good meal for the rats!" Joseph utters these last words in a comical tone; his expression is quite funny, and we all burst out laughing—even Kazik, whose laughter turns immediately to violent coughing.

"It was Kazik's coughing that brought you here, isn't that so?"

"Yes," I say. I realize that the four of them

are very glad to see us. I too rejoice at having met them. In such circumstances friendship is quickly born.

"Did you realize there was someone on the other side of the canal?" Isaac asks.

"Of course," Joseph replies. "But we thought it was the Germans."

Again Kazik is seized by a fit of violent coughing. As soon as it stops, Joseph goes on with his story.

"Yes, we thought it was no longer necessary to stay on guard. We were going to lie down, when a new sound reached our ears—a sound different from the previous one. It was as though someone was scratching the ground. At the same time, we noticed in the distance a faint light. This time we were absolutely sure that some plot was being hatched against us, that they wanted to attack us from both sides of the canal. We told ourselves, They withdraw from one side, in order to advance from the other, but when Kazik coughed again, and even dropped something with a noise which seemed to reecho even more loudly since all was so quiet, we noticed that on the other side they had put out their light, too, while one man who was alone quickly ran away. This time we were quite bewildered and asked ourselves, What does all this senseless coming and going signify? Are they Germans or devils?

"Naturally, that night, contrary to our custom, we didn't put on any light. We waited in the dark." Joseph shows us a lamp surrounded by thick paper which serves as a shade. "With this lamp we hardly run the risk of being seen. But that time we were afraid to use it at all." He is thoughtful for a moment, then he puts his hand on Isaac's shoulder and exclaims with a bitter smile; "Hell, it's not enough to be afraid of the Germans, we have to tremble before each other as well."

The night will soon be over. We have to make our way back while it is still dark. And we are in a hurry to break the good news to our companions, to tell them they have nothing to fear. Before leaving our new friends, we briefly relate our own story and invite them to visit our bunker and celebrate our meeting by taking a meal with us.

They accept our invitation with visible pleasure. Kazik even jokes and promises us he will not cough anymore so as not to frighten us. We take leave of each other very cordially.

Our return is a very gay one. We quite forget that we are in a underground canal which is filthy and odorous. We go as quickly as we can and are soon near the opening of the bunker, where Ignace is on guard.

"Well?" he says impatiently. "Who is it? Tell us quickly."

In a few word we satisfy his curiosity, then we climb toward the bunker to givc more details to our companions. Daniel has preceded us and approaches Hannah and tells her rapidly about our discovery. Hannah listens to him, delighted; her face beams, she smiles with pleasure, and her eyes shine with joy. Daniel and the others are smiling. Hannah and Samek hastily prepare something for us to eat. Then we lie down, relaxed and happy, thinking of the imaginary danger and of the celebration we shall have tomorrow.

The following night when Joseph makes his way into our bunker followed by his three friends—preceded by Daniel, who went to show them the way—his first words are:

"God in heaven! It's quite a palace you've got here."

Our bunker has been decked out for a celebration. Today Haskel did not go with the others to search in the cellars. He said he did not feel well. But when we came back from our foraging expedition, we found a narrow table pushed against a wall and near the table, a bench.

Haskel made the table and bench out of some planks which were piled up in the bunker to serve as fuel for the fire. Using a stone, he removed all the nails; then he fastened two planks together, added another plank at each side, nailed it all together—and our table was ready.

"When you have guests, you've got to make the house look nice," Haskel tells us.

We are all in such high spirits that we do not even feel we are in a bunker. Hannah is flushed with emotion, as befits the mistress of the house, who wants the meal to be successful and pleasing to the guests. Samek hovers around her, somewhat solemn, helpful, an agreeable smile on his lips.

Daniel does not understand Polish, but the happy expression on his face speaks for itself. Of all the four, Joseph is the most garrulous. It is he who introduces his friends.

"The little one over there is called Wozniak. He's a carpenter. He lived quite near here with his mother who died when the city was being bombed during the insurrection. The tall one over there is called Antek. He used to work in the fields with his father in a village near Warsaw. He left his wife and child there, and he came here to help us drive out the Germans. The one with the cough is called Kazik; he seems to be an intellectual." And Joseph adds, laughing: "It's only thanks to him that we're alive. He never stops praying. Let him pray as much as he likes, all well and good. But I must admit that he was a great help in thrashing the Germans."

Hannah, always the perfect hostess, invites everyone to take his place, and the party begins. For each one Hannah has prepared a little cake made with a handful of the flour found in a cellar mixed with a little water and cooked on hot bricks. Then she places on the table a saucepan full of "soup"—that is to say, hot water in which here and there a few bits of pasta, made with the same flour, float. Hannah announces proudly that the water from which the soup is made came from the spring that was discovered the night before. We wish each other a speedy liberation, and our thoughts fly across the Vistula toward Praga and the Red Army.

Joseph, who has remained pensive for a moment, exclaims: "Aie, such a celebration, and not a single drop of brandy."

"We'll make up for it," Isaac consoles him, "when we get out of here. Then we'll get drunk, good and proper!"

"Yes, we'll get drunk all right!" Ignace repeats. "We'll have to, so as not to go out of our minds when we see all the ruins."

"We're having a party tonight!" Hannah retorts, almost angry. "Tonight at least don't think of the world above us; let's just be happy we're here."

So we begin to enjoy our soup, which is really hot, and Joseph compliments Hannah several times on her good cooking. Hannah blushes a little, but she is very pleased. We are all in high spirits. We are like relatives gathered together for a family celebration. The bunker resounds with our laughter. The soup and the little cakes are much appreciated. Every face reflects the party mood.

We listen to our new friends, who tell us about the fighting during the insurrection. Although this is not a new subject to us, we listen to them with interest, for each one of us has lived through these moments differently and has reacted to these events in his own way. So, in imagination, we once more live through this unforgettable time.

Little Wozniak tells the story of the battle he witnessed. As he speaks, he gesticulates in a lively manner, not only with his hands but with all his body, as though he is fighting again.

"When our group first attacked the German detachment stationed near us in Freta Street, it was nearly five o'clock in the afternoon. It was the first of August, a Tuesday, I think. The Germans were so taken by surprise that they hardly put up any resistance. Some of them ran away and probably fell into the hands of another group of insurgents who were quite near, since the insurrection broke out at the same time in all districts of Warsaw. Many Germans surrendered immediately. People came out into the streets to see what was going on. Some of them were terrified and went back and shut themselves up indoors. Others joined our ranks. They helped us barricade the streets and alleys which led to the Vistula. Our group was sent to the corner of Sierakowska Street, where we joined other groups and began to get ready to attack Danzig Station. The first night was calm, and the next day many streets were in our hands. The population was jubilant. Groups of musicians wandered around the town, playing their instruments.

"Very late at night, after a whole day of preparation, we began to approach Danzig Station on many sides at oncc. We were already very close to it when, abruptly, sustained gunfire stopped our advance. After two hours, we had to withdraw with heavy losses. But—a strange thing—once we had drawn back, the Germans did not pursue us. We learned later that they were fortifying their positions near the Vistula so as to be able not only to make a stand there but also to go on the attack."

"The population's joy was short-lived," interrupts Joseph.

"The fourth day of the insurrection, the Germans showed us what they could do," Wozniak went on. "From their airplanes they threw leaflets which called on us to surrender. Naturally, we didn't. The fifth day they threw down leaflets again, renewing their call. Then they employed their old, tried-and-true method of turning one part of the population against the other. Certain planes flooded the town with special leaflets in which they threatened the population with reprisals, and at the same time they advised them not to let themselves be led by the Jews and Communists who had escaped from camps and taken command of the uprising.

"This time nobody was taken in. This was because we had really seen them—these Jews in their striped prison clothes right out of the camps—we had really seen them fighting beside us and falling like heroes. No one thought of surrendering," affirms Wozniak, almost shouting.

"Then they started bombing the city, destroying it, beginning with the Old Town.

"Once," continues Wozniak, lowering his voice, "I ran home after such a bombardment to see my mother. I found the house in ruins and all the people who lived in it buried underneath, including my mother."

He turns away from us and quickly, so we will not notice it—for he doesn't wish to spoil our festivity—he touches a finger to the tear running down his cheek. He forces himself to smile, but the atmosphere of gaiety is already destroyed. It is sufficient to say only one word and thousands of mothers rise up in the bunker and stand in front of us. Then the bunker becomes a bunker again.

It is late, the night is reaching its end. Joseph and his companions are ready to leave. They regret that time has passed so quickly, they have so much more still to tell us about the revolt.

"We'll come again tomorrow," Wozniak says. "We know the way now."

Isaac suggests that they stay with us. True, there is not much room in our bunker, but we could manage. They thank us effusively but decline our offer, for all sorts of reasons. First of all, there is hardly any room; then, they are afraid of German bombs, which can fall at any moment on our bunker and destroy it. Down there in the canal they are more sheltered; moreover, they are seeking a way of leaving Warsaw for one of the surrounding villages. If they manage to get out of the city they will not have to be afraid anymore, since they are Polish.

They take their leave of us with great cordiality, pass one by one into the underground passage, and from there they go down into the canal. Only one of them stays with us—Kazik. We do not let him go back, for he is coughing and would not last long down there. We prepare a place for him, and he lies down. Covering his mouth with his hand, he tries to stifle his coughing. Intensive firing tells us it is time for us to lie down too: it is already daylight. We put out the lamp and each of us goes to his place.

No one sleeps. Ignace is more afraid than usual, and when the throbbing of aircraft is heard he starts up and remains in a sitting position. When the noise comes quite close, he falls back, pressing himself against the ground, as though he wants to hide in it, to take shelter right inside it.

Hannah twists and turns on her couch. Without any doubt she is thinking of her mother. When Wozniak told us how his mother perished, we all noticed Hannah's face suddenly change. The smile disappeared. When Hannah first entered the bunker, she had lost track of her mother. Perhaps her mother too was the victim of a bombardment. In the bunker, one word, an allusion, is sufficient to chase away the gaiety which occasionally comes to us in moments of forgetfulness. Hannah tosses on her couch and starts at every exploding shell. She is crying softly.

For a long time I lie awake listening to the artillery. I do not fall asleep until very late. When I open my eyes again, Hannah is already up. She is heating a little water for Kazik, whose coughing is obviously exhausting him. Hannah's face betrays nothing of her recent emotion. She is calm and is once more smiling her usual smile. As always, she wishes those of us who are going outside a speedy, safe return. This way Hannah has of blessing us before we go out has become a tradition; each time we go to explore the cellars we are not at all certain of coming back.

With Haskel I go down into the canal to get water from our spring. "This time, I'll stay as long as necessary and bring back a huge basin of water," Haskel says, making his way toward the canal. "It will be possible to have a real good wash!"

"Try and find us a bar of soap," I say to Isaac, who is getting ready to go out with Daniel.

Samek and Ignace follow them. Kazik remains in the bunker with Hannah.

Waiting for hours on end in the canal until the water from the tiny spring fills our receptacles is the most difficult thing for me to do. I stand in one spot in a darkness so thick that it hurts my eyes; the distant sound of water gives the impression of endless waves cascading one after the other in a deafening resonance. But each of us in turn must accept the weary task of getting water; and, in the end, we more or less get used to it.

It is very late when Haskel and I return to the bunker. Isaac and Daniel are already there and did not come back empty-handed. Under some bricks and stones they found a parcel filled with shirts and underwear. They could not have found anything better.

From the very beginning of our underground existence we have been satisfied with very little; as soon as we unearth anything during our foraging expeditions, we carry it back immediately to the bunker and seek nothing more. We live from day to day, thinking that the start of the Russian offensive is imminent and consequently that unless we die in the course of the fighting (which is, after all, quite possible), we shall be liberated.

And so here we are, in great good humor. We have brought water. "After dinner," Hannah says, "I shall clean myself up; and you will clean yourselves too. Afterwards each of you will put on a clean shirt. You will look like princes," she says, laughing, and begins to prepare the meal.

But soon our good mood disappears. Samek and Ignace, who have both gone to explore the cellars, have not yet returned. It is only toward dawn, when we are convinced we will never see them again, that Hannah, standing close to the entrance waiting for Samek, hears the sound of footsteps climbing toward our bunker.

"They're here!" she shouts, then jumps aside to leave the passage clear.

Samek and Ignace can scarcely walk. Their faces are so covered with mud and dust it is difficult to recognize them. They are on the point of exhaustion.

"We were just about to come back," Samek says, "and we were bringing some good things —some kidney beans and a few potatoes. I was saying to Ignace: 'What a meal we'll have today, a real feast! I'm very fond of potatoes.' Suddenly, we heard footsteps coming from the yard we had to cross. Then we heard voices, words in German. It was two sentries! We made our way into another yard, so we could hide in the ruins. As we were running into a ruined house, we began to climb over a pile of debris. Then everything collapsed under us, and we found ourselves in a cellar beneath a pile of stones. We were terribly afraid; the Germans could quite easily have heard the noise. So we stayed there, until we were sure the Germans weren't coming after us. Then, when we were ready to start back, we found we were buried beneath this pile of debris and were unable to free ourselves."

"We thought we'd never get out," Ignace interrupts.

"Each time we tried to climb up the side, we would fall back into the hole again. We finally managed it. But we were not able to save the potatoes!"

"The main thing is that you're here," said Hannah, helping Samek to clean the dirt off himself. "Now let's all sit down at the table."

She is very happy. What a wonderful girl she is, our Hannah! So friendly, so kind to everyone of us—a born optimist. Only when she remembers her mother does she become sad. At such times, she lies down, closes her eyes, and pretends to be asleep.

Now, after Samek's return, she is as playful as a child. She talks to us of her childhood and is pleased when we listen. Her features are relaxed, her eyes shine. I suspect that she wants, at this moment, to forget the bunker and to transport herself to the spacious drawing room of her house in Lodz at 27 Zeromski Street, where she spent her earliest years and where she was able to satisfy all the whims of a rich young girl.

"I was the only daughter of rich parents, and I was very spoiled," she says, smiling. "My father had a textile factory. Besides mama, who constantly took great care of me, I had a governess from early childhood, and I never lacked for anything. In our house we didn't speak Yiddish. I went to a private school. When anti-Semitism increased in Poland, especially just before the war, it didn't affect me personally. My parents thought a child should not know about such things. They thought that anti-Semitism would die a natural death, that it didn't really concern them, and that their little Hannah would never be affected by it."

Hannah turns toward Samek, ponders a moment, and then smiles. "Once when I was rushing down some stairs—I was already a big girl—I bumped into a boy. He fell and dropped the satchel he was carrying. He was older than I. I was afraid, thinking he'd hurt himself, and I began to apologize to him. He looked at me and said: 'Don't worry about it, you have to laugh and run around when you're young; you never know what will happen later.' He said it with such a serious manner that I thought about it for a long time after the incident. For some days, whenever I came back from school and climbed the stairs, I would look around to see if I hadn't been followed. I began to think about him all the time. I reproached myself for doing so, but it didn't do any good.

"Once when I was on our balcony, I noticed him just across the way. He was sitting on a third floor balcony, reading a book. He saw me too and our eyes met. I was embarrassed and my heart started to beat rapidly. The boy spoke to me; I replied. Mama, who was in her room and heard me speaking, came and joined me. 'Who are you talking to, Hannah?' she asked. I was embarrassed and didn't know how to reply." Now Hannah laughs. "You know very well who this boy was," she says. "There he is, there—he's called Samek." She goes up to Samek, who kisses her.

Throughout this whole story, Daniel has never taken his eyes off Hannah; now he lowers his head. I glance at him, then at the girl, and I think she has done the right thing—to speak openly and sincerely of her love for Samek, so as not to give Daniel any false hopes.

Then Ignace, who is on guard at the bunker opening, reminds us it is time to go to sleep.

Many dangers threaten us here: discovery by the Germans; death from shells or bombs; hunger; disease as a result of the filth around us, the ground we lie on, the smells coming from the sewers, the corpses strewn throughout the debris. To all this, there is now added yet another torment: the flies.

It is summer; we wallow in filth; we are near the sewers—and so dense swarms of flies buzz around the bunker. During the "day," when we remain lying in the darkness, we hear such buzzing that terror takes hold of us. And as soon as the fire is lit they descend on us. They get inside our ears, our nostrils, our mouths. Our lives are one great struggle against them.

The greatest difficulty arises when we are having our meal. With one hand we have to protect our food so the flies will not get to it and with the other, our faces. Each of us has adopted his own particular method of combatting this scourge. Sometimes these methods are so peculiar and give us such a comical appearance that we cannot help laughing. For us to be able to laugh is an infinitely precious thing. We need laughter almost as much as we need food and drink.

Ignace wraps his face and head in a duster, in which he has made two little holes for the eyes and another for the nose and mouth. Masked in this fashion, he walks among us. The sight of him arouses laughter. And we can't help laughing when we see how Haskel, armed with a rag, chases the flies toward the canal. For to judge from his expression he seems to be imploring them: "Haven't we enough misfortune without you? Must you add to our misery?" When he sees that neither the rag nor his supplications are effective, he gets angry, and addresses the most murderous insults to the flies.

It is at these moments that Hannah, smilingly, has to say to him: "Mr. Haskel, flies do *not* understand Yiddish!"

And everyone, including Haskel, starts laughing heartily.

And yet most of the time we could weep. When it comes to the flies, we have no defense; and we have no means of fighting them. One day we try a concerted attack; we start chasing them toward the canal. Having succeeded in getting rid of them, we cover the entrance to the canal with a piece of cloth so they will not be able to return. But we cannot stay shut in like this for long. Soon we are short of air, and we are forced to removed the cloth. Immediately the flies swarm back into the bunker. More than once we are forced to put out the fire and remain in darkness in order to be able to breathe a little.

Only much later, when the first cold spell starts, will the flies finally disappear.

Our bunker population has increased by one. The first day, Kazik hardly takes any part in our life. He watches us, carefully, somewhat suspiciously. His face betrays a certain anguish. Had he been in good health, he would certainly not have joined us. But he had no choice. He could not have stayed any longer in the canal; he would have died there. So he remains with us and watches us.

We force ourselves to speak Polish as much as possible so that he will understand us. His behavior makes it very clear that he has never lived among Jews and has probably never known any Jews. That is why we do not ask him too many questions. We want him to get used to us. In our turn, we watch him too, but we try not to make it noticeable.

From his behavior and manners, we assume he is an intellectual. His language is that of an educated man. His comrades in the canal have told us that he is a strange man; he never talks about himself. They even joked about him and claimed he is always praying. Lying now in our bunker, watching us, coughing from time to time, Kazik is something of a mystery.

It is by pure chance that we finally discover who he really is.

One evening we are preparing ourselves for our usual foraging expedition when we see Kazik trying to get up. He removes the coat that covers him, stands up, and begins to fold it. A small briefcase falls out of the coat, and all the papers in it are scattered about. We notice a photograph of a man in a cassock.

Kazik quickly picks up the papers, but he

realizes we have seen the photograph. His face reddens, and he looks at us with embarrassment and a little fear. For a moment no one knows what to say, so great is our surprise. A priest among us!

Kazik is the first to break the silence.

"Here I am not a priest," he declares. "Here I am just like all of you, a man fleeing from the same enemy!" He seems to be a little afraid of us.

"The fact that you are a priest doesn't matter," Isaac assures him. "You needn't be afraid of us because we're Jews."

"No," says Kazik, "that's not what I meant. I am trying to make you understand that here I should like to be the same as all of you, to go out with you to look for food and to work like you."

"But you are ill," Hannah remarks, addressing him respectfully. Kazik again protests; he insists that we continue to call him Kazik and not Casimir, which is his Christian name; he insists that he be treated exactly like all the other comrades.

We cannot continue the conversation, for at night each minute is precious. Haskel takes the bucket and goes down to the canal to get water. Samek and Ignace go out to explore the cellars. Daniel and Isaac follow them.

It is my turn to remain in the bunker and help Hannah with her preparations. Kazik, breathing with difficulty, lies down again, covers himself with his coat, and coughs a little. I do not talk to him, although I would like to ask him thousands of questions. How is it that he is here? What are the reasons for it? What does he think of the Jews? The fear he showed when we discovered he was a priest makes me suspect that he does not feel quite at ease as regards Jews. But there is a tradition in our bunker, an unwritten law that all of us observe: when someone is outside the bunker risking his life on a foraging expedition in the cellars and ruins, those who are inside await his return in almost absolute silence, without exchanging an unnecessary word. Thus a link is maintained between all of us. Only when everybody is back together again is there relaxation and talk.

Immediately upon his return, Ignace asks: "How is the priest?" It seems he has found some cough medicine. He pulls it from his pocket wrapped up in a bit of rag and grins broadly, very pleased with his find. "You see, I found some Liptov tea, very good for coughs!"

It is Ignace who is most attached to the priest, although all of us, without exception, do our best to make him feel that he is not a stranger among us.

Later, when we are all seated at the table, the relaxed atmosphere of friendship has its effect upon the priest, and he begins to confide in us.

"I've never mixed with Jews; I've never had any dealings with them at all. We lived in a village near Treblinka. My parents used to work in the fields. We were not really poor. I was the youngest child in the family. My family was religious; we were Catholics. When I told my parents I wanted to become a priest they were very happy. At the grammar school and later at the seminary in Warsaw, I took no interest in anything outside my studies. It was only when I began to carry out my duties as a priest that I took any interest in real life."

"Didn't you hear about anti-Semitism?" Isaac asks him.

Kazik turns to Isaac. "To tell you the truth, before the war, the problem of anti-Semitism didn't interest me. As I already told you, I had never been near any Jews. Of course, I saw some in the streets of Warsaw and Lodz where I often went, but that was all. They were completely unknown to me. And to be absolutely honest, perhaps I even told myself when I read articles in the press attacking the Jews that if they are always being persecuted, there must be good reasons for it." Kazik speaks more slowly, as if weighing each of his words. "I want you to understand that when I thought of Jews I did not hate them. As a devout Catholic, I couldn't hate anyone; that would have been a crime. But I didn't like them either. The majority were like me. They didn't like the Jews, although they had no specific reason to dislike them. They didn't know why they didn't like them; but most of them didn't want to harm the Jews or even help the anti-Semites."

I interrupt him here. "That attitude helped make Hitler's work a lot easier."

"That's true," Kazik replies. "But I only understood that later—too late!"

Then he tells us how he joined the insurrection.

"One day I had to go to Lodz on parish business. I saw armed Germans driving people from the streets, and soon I noticed four men walking in the middle of the road, their hands in the air, surrounded by Germans with machine guns in their hands. When they had gone, I asked someone who these men were and where they were being taken. He told me they were members of the Polish Resistance movement who had been caught and were probably going to be shot."

"I returned home and thought of what I'd seen and heard in Lodz. When I gave my sermon the following Sunday, I made it quite clear to my parishioners that it was their duty to resist the invader. I began to influence people to join the Resistance. Finally, I had to flee from my village. I went to Warsaw, exchanged my cassock for civilian clothes, and became one of the Resistance fighters. During the uprising I was stationed in Kozla Street, but I fought in other places as well."

Kazik seems to acquire new life as he talks about his comrades-in-arms; he knows many interesting things about the uprising, and these in the greatest detail. But we are forced to put off the rest of his story until later. The artillery has begun; day has come. For us, it is night, and we must now sleep.

six

But I am unable to sleep. I think of the part that Jews took in the uprising led by Bor-Komorowski and the attitude of the Polish fighters toward them. I see Jewish fighters murdered by their own comrades-in-arms—killed purely and simply because they are Jews. The memory of this has a profound influence on me and weakens the sense of comradeship I have for the Poles in the Resistance movement.

Of course, I realize that the majority of Polish fighters were loyal and friendly toward us: the Jew-killers were only a small minority. Nevertheless, in my present situation the memory of these killers fills me with anger and pain.

Now, lying on the ground in our bunker, I recall the early days of the uprising when hundreds of Jews who had been brought to Warsaw by the Nazis—and hundreds of others who had found refuge in the "Aryan" part of the city—flung themselves into the battle.

At the beginning of the uprising we happened to be in Mlawska Street, and like everybody else we put up barricades to prevent the Germans from capturing our positions. Though weakened by years of living in concentration camps, we worked as hard as any of the others.

One night toward midnight we were lying in a yard in that same street. It was an enormous yard. There were many Jews there at that particular moment, waiting to be assigned to various combat areas. We had spent an exhausting day building barricades; now we were stretched out on the ground, dozing. An officer arrived. Everyone had to wake up.

"I need twelve men for a dangerous mission." He spoke quietly and slowly. "Twelve men. I don't want to choose them myself. I want volunteers."

Twelve Jews leaped up. I was one of them. We left the yard and followed the officer through a network of alleyways, the names of which we didn't even know. But we realized that we were making our way toward the Vistula.

Occasionally Germans would fire on us from the windows of houses. We reached the designated area late that night. The officer stationed us at the corner of a street. In the distance we could see an empty square behind which flowed the Vistula. In the last house on the street, picks, shovels, and other implements were waiting for us, together with two machine guns.

"There you are," the officer said to us. "It's a case of digging trenches here, but in such a fashion that the Germans won't be able to see them. Two of you carrying machine guns will mount guard on the ten comrades digging the trenches. Don't forget, the Germans are very near here; not only can they fire on you from their observation posts, they can even attack you. So you'll have to work carefully, without making any noise—and very, very quickly. The trenches must be ready before daybreak."

Ten of us picked up shovels and started to work feverishly. The officer seemed astonished to find such strength left in people who had come from ghettos and concentration camps. It was the desire to fight against the hated enemy that gave us our strength.

Before daybreak, the trenches and barricades were ready for the combatants who were to repulse the German attacks. The Nazis wanted to carve their way toward the Old Town, and it was imperative for them to take this strategic point.

Very early in the morning, the officer went back with us to our yard in Mlawska Street. He said to the lieutenant on guard: "Heroes! That's what they are!"

Then he cordially shook hands with us and left. Almost dead with fatigue, we sank to the ground and immediately fell asleep. . . .

Another time we were occupying a building on Okopowa Street. We put up a barricade in the yard and in that way succeeded in cutting the Germans off from their reinforcements. We realized the Germans attached great importance to the position we were defending, for they attacked us without respite. We had been hanging on to it for several days under extremely difficult conditions. There were forty-four of us; six were Jews.

One morning the Germans attacked in force. Lying behind our barricade, we saw a German detachment armed with automatic weapons advancing toward us, covered by sustained gunfire from other German formations concealed behind them. We could not withdraw, for in that case they would have killed us all. Our situation had become desperate; our lieutenant already envisaged surrender.

During the uprising the Germans did not always execute their prisoners, for they wanted to convince the Resistance fighters of their humane feelings and of the uselessness of the insurrection. But we Jews knew exactly how things stood for us and what we could expect from the Germans. So we decided not to let ourselves be taken alive.

Before we could express our thoughts to the lieutenant, one of us climbed over the barricade and raced toward the Germans, shouting and firing. The Polish-made automatic weapons were excellent. The rest of the Jews immediately rushed after him, firing at the Germans. Encouraged by the example of the six Jews, all the other Resistance fighters rushed forward, with the result that the surprised and frightened Germans immediately withdrew to their fortified positions.

Our lieutenant took advantage of the situation to order our safe withdrawal; so we were able to leave our position and even take with us our three dead and five seriously wounded. One of the wounded and two of the dead were Jews. . . .

I remember the Jew I came across in Mlawska Street. We were in an enormous yard that had been destroyed to such a point that it opened into other yards and even onto the street. Standing one day with the lieutenant and other comrades in front of the entrance to this yard, I heard shooting, and suddenly I saw a man on the ground in the last convulsions of death. Then I saw a second man calmly putting his gun back in his holster. He marched up to us with a confident step, like a hunter who has just killed a rabbit. On reaching us, he saluted the lieutenant and said to him with a smile: "To hell with him, he was a Jew!" Then off he went.

The lieutenant looked at me, read the emotion on my face, and explained, as though wanting to apologize to me for taking no action: "I couldn't do anything; he wasn't in my platoon!"

It is possible that he really could do nothing. No doubt he himself would not have raised his hand against a Jew; but I am quite sure that he had no feeling of kindness for us. He and our priest are of the same kind.

I went up to the Jew who had just been killed.

He was a tall, strong-looking man of about forty. He lay with his eyes open. An expression of pain still sharpened his features. He must have realized that his murderer was not a German but a Pole, one of his comrades-in-arms, a man he had regarded as a friend. Then I got up and gazed at the ruins of Warsaw. Wounded comrades lay everywhere in the rubble. Their cries reached us clearly. If I had believed in God, I would have said that He had punished Warsaw because of all those Polish cutthroats for whom the murder of millions of Jews was still not enough and who took the lives of those few who had escaped, those few for whom it might have been possible to see the end of the war and rejoice in the liberation. . . .

Now I am in Miodowa Street. It is the very beginning of the uprising. We are putting up the barricades. Everyone is mobilized. We tear up stones, pull doors off their old iron hinges. Everyone helps. They say the Germans are approaching from the Cracovian Suburb—they must not pass!

The entire population—those who favored the uprising and those who did not—is now unified. We must all fight the Germans! Everyone does what he can. The barricades grow larger. The Jews from the concentration camps—we are still wearing our striped prison clothing—work feverishly.

The combatants begin to muster. When the firing gets closer, unarmed men and women take refuge in the cellars. Those who are armed lie behind the barricades and open fire on the approaching Germans. There is a rain of bullets on our trenches. The first of our wounded are taken away; the first of our dead litter the pavements. But after awhile we force the enemy to withdraw. Despite the wounded and dead, the joy of victory takes hold of all of us.

About twenty Jews take part in the battle. I am helping bring in the dead and wounded when I hear a shout.

"Jews! Jews! S.o.b.'s!"

Shots ring out and two Jews in striped clothing fall. Near them are two men, weapons in hand, shouting:

"We don't need Jews! They should all be wiped out!"

They look at the rows of wounded, as if searching for other Jews to kill. Boiling with rage, some of us are just about to pounce on them; but some Poles surround them and drag them away.

Other Jews suffer the same fate. Many Poles have begun a Jew hunt on the barricades. And for a long time cries of "Death to the Jews!" mingle with the joyous cries of the insurgents as all of us watch the enemy retreat. . . .

seven

I fall into a heavy sleep. When I open my eyes I see Haskel is already up. He is waiting for the firing to stop completely so as to be able to go and get water from our spring.

He lights the lamp and mutters between his teeth. We know that for some days now he has been obsessed by a terrible anxiety: he is afraid that the spring may be drying up and that we will be without fresh water once more. The fear of this weighs upon all of us. From the moment Haskel told us that the water no longer flows regularly drop by drop but stops now and then, we have all been worried about it. Yet no one takes it to heart as much as Haskel. The spring has a kind of fascination for him.

Today Haskel has risen a little earlier than usual. He takes the bucket, the pot, matches, and a candle; then he goes down into the underground passage. We all get up to get ready for our individual tasks. Suddenly we hear Haskel crawling rapidly back toward us. We stiffen with fear. Soon Haskel reappears in the opening; he looks terrified. "Quiet, everyone; put out the light!"

In a whisper he tells us that while he was waiting for the pot to fill he suddenly heard footsteps behind him. So he grabbed the bucket and pot and came back to the bunker. But behind him he had made out the glow of a flashlight turned in his direction. He flattened himself against the wall. The light seemed to come from a long way off, and soon it was extinguished. Then, still skirting the wall, he made his way back to us.

Isaac and I go down into the canal opening. For some minutes we stay there, listening. We hear nothing. I am convinced that Haskel is mistaken. Is he not constantly obsessed by the fear of being caught? But suddenly a ray of light appears in the canal opening; then it goes out. And we hear the steps of several people. This time there is no doubt; they are searching for us!

The footsteps in the canal become more and more pronounced. The walls magnify their muffled tread. The light is much brighter. Suddenly the steps cease. The light is trained on the opening to our bunker. They have spotted our hole! How long do we wait?

A cry rings out in Polish: "Who's there?"

Isaac and I immediately reply in Polish: "Your comrades!"

"Come out or we fire!" a peremptory voice commands.

The fact that this order is in Polish and not in German is reassuring. We come out—Isaac first and then me. A strong, blinding light is trained upon us. Only when they turn the light away can we make out three men in single file, their automatic weapons pointed at us. They are wearing Polish Army caps and waterproof clothing suitable for the descent into the sewer. They all have armbands bearing the letters A.K. [*Armia Krajowa*], the badge of the National Polish Liberation Army.

One of them asks: "Who are you and what are you doing here?"

"We are Jews," Isaac says. "We were in the insurrection, and now we are hiding in a bunker."

They look at each other for a moment. Then the one who spoke to us and who seems to be the leader says with a smile: "We thought you were Germans. It's a good thing you came out and showed yourselves. We were just going to throw a grenade in here. Are you alone?"

"There are eight of us," replies Isaac.

The leader of the group has a short conversation with his comrades, then turns to us.

"Listen, we're from Zoliborz. The struggle is still going on there. We've come down here to try and find a passage which will lead us to the Vistula. We have to know what's going on there, what forces the Germans have at their disposal. We're trying to get there through the canal because the Germans control all the routes on the surface. We'll be coming back this way in a few hours. If you want to, you can join us. But to tell you the truth, we don't know how long we'll be able to hold out, and the road through the canal is not easy."

Then they walk away. Isaac and I go back into the bunker. Our comrades are aware that the men are Poles; they have heard part of our conversation. We explain the proposal that has been made to us; but for the moment no one can decide on the best course of action to take. It is not easy to make such a decision. And the words of the leader, "We don't know how long we'll be able to hold out," have a depressing effect on us.

But I make up my mind to join the insurgents —to become once more a part of the living world, to get out of this tomb. The idea is so tempting that I don't even want to think of what might happen later. Yet I say nothing. I do not want to influence anyone. Each one must do exactly what he thinks best.

Time goes by; soon the insurgents will be returning. At last Ignace makes up his mind.

"I'm staying here. I'm no good for anything, whatever happens."

Immediately Haskel says: "I don't trust anybody, Germans or Poles."

Isaac says, softly: "To die here or there . . . what's the difference? So why make the long journey?"

Hannah looks at Samek.

"You wouldn't have the strength to keep up with them," Samek says.

Both of them hang their heads.

"I would go," our priest, Kazik, says, starting to cough, "but how can I?"

I remain silent but start getting ready. I tuck the legs of my trousers into my socks and I tie strings around the socks. I tighten my shoelaces so they'll keep firm around my ankles. I tuck my jacket into my trousers and tighten the belt; I have to be prepared to march through water and mud.

When Daniel sees that I am getting ready to go, he does the same. As though apologizing to the others, he says: "We were together in the camp and in Warsaw. We were always together. He's like a father to me. If he goes, I'm going too."

There is a noise outside; someone is coming into the underground passage. It is our Polish friends: Joseph, Antek, and Wozniak. They too have been discovered by the insurgents' patrol and have decided to go with them.

The patrol returns. We say our good-byes. We must reach Zoliborz before daybreak. The five kilometers we have to walk in the canal will be long indeed.

Hannah tries hard not to cry, but tears shine in her eyes. For a long time we embrace our companions. The priest crosses himself and begins to pray for us. Daniel glances repeatedly at Hannah but says nothing.

Ignace is the last to say good-bye to us. He

slips a bit of chalk into my hand.

"Mark the way," he advises me. "Perhaps you will be forced to come back."

"You can be sure of one thing," I tell them. "If things up there are better than they are here, we shall come back for you."

One by one we climb through the underground passage toward the canal. Daniel brings up the rear; it is obviously difficult for him to leave the bunker.

When we reach the canal, we arrange ourselves in single file. The leader of the patrol, a sergeant, asks us where the others are. I explain the situation to him. Shrugging his shoulders, he says to me: "Perhaps it is they who are right."

He gives us instructions: at all costs we must avoid making any noise; we must not stamp our feet on the ground or utter a single word; each time we pass beneath a sewer grating leading outside the canal, we must be doubly cautious because these points are often manned by German sentries, who might easily hear the noise of our footsteps. In places where the water and mud make it particularly difficult to walk, we must hold on to the man in front of us with one hand, and with the other support ourselves by holding on to the wall.

After giving us our instructions, the sergeant orders us to follow him. We move very slowly, making the least noise possible. We are walking against the current and have to muster all our strength in order to go forward at all. Although the man at the head of the line has a flashlight, he is afraid the Germans might discover the light, so he uses it only when we are halfway between two sewer exits, to see if anyone is missing. In the canal, the darkness is very different from that in the outside world. In a field, even in a wood, you can get used to the darkness and even manage to see a little bit, because a certain luminosity persists. It is quite different in the canal, which is built of concrete and shut in on all sides. The darkness there is total; you imagine you can touch it with your fingers.

I think to myself that this is a darkness like the one blind people experience. Indeed, I can manage better with my eyes closed than with them open, for it is precisely then that I have the feeling of being able to see nothing at all. With my eyes closed, I find the darkness more natural, and walking is easier for me. As we gradually move forward, the noise of our footsteps is less pronounced; the water is deeper, and from time to time it even comes up to our knees and higher. The only noise I can hear is the lapping of the waters as we go forward against the current. Occasionally I have the feeling I am no longer walking but being carried forward by the water. The sound of the rushing waves beats like a hammer in my head. Minutes begin to seem like hours. I feel as though I have been walking for an eternity.

We reach a crossing where the canals empty into the principal canal. The sergeant stops, lights his flashlight, and directs us toward the middle canal and from there toward the main one. At each crossing, I make a big white cross with my bit of chalk, so that if necessary we can make our way back to our bunker. After two hours of walking in this way, Daniel and I are exhausted; it would not take much for my young comrade to fall and disappear in this filthy water.

At last the sergeant suggests that we stop and rest a little. We press ourselves against the wall so that the current cannot carry us off.

"Cheer up," the sergeant says. "We've already come halfway. We'll soon be there." With his flashlight, he lights the way, and we see before us muddy waves jostling each other with an infernal roar and flinging themselves upon us. I look at Daniel, who is clinging to me, and recall the sergeant's words about our companions in the bunker: "Perhaps it is they who are right." I now no longer doubt that they have acted very reasonably. I do not believe I shall ever reach Zoliborz.

When the sergeant orders us to set off again, I am not so much walking as dragging myself along. Young Daniel guesses this, takes my two hands, places them on his shoulders, and hoists me up. But after a minute or two I realize that by allowing this, I shall be dragging Daniel down with me to his death. I force myself to see my wife and two sons, to imagine their joy at our reunion. As if by magic, my weakness passes. I am not tired anymore.

A thousand tiny lights are suddenly before us. They belong to the Resistance fighters from Zoliborz. The sentries see us.

"Halt!"

Daniel is breathing heavily. Turning his head toward me, he smiles; but I realize he can hardly stand up.

The patrol gives the password; the sentries let us through. We have reached the end of the canal. We climb through an opening and are now outside. But this last effort exhausts me completely. I lie down on the ground. Two soldiers come up and help me to my feet; they hold me up, so that I can go with my comrades into a nearby house.

We enter a huge room with many doors. I realize that we are in the headquarters of the Zoliborz district Resistance fighters. Soon a door opens and an officer appears. He is an elderly man, short in stature, with fine features. He looks like an intellectual. Behind him comes the patrol which brought us. For a moment the officer looks at Daniel and me silently. Our clothes are dripping with water and mud, our faces are pale and gaunt after so many months spent in camps and in fighting and three weeks of living underground. In a pleasant manner, the officer asks us where we come from and what circumstances forced us to take refuge in the bunker.

"I come from Paris and from Auschwitz," I tell him.

Immediately he sends for a woman of about forty who smiles at us and says in good French:

"Come with me. First of all, you'd better clean up a little. Then we'll have a chat and you'll tell me who you are."

Before taking leave of us, the officer tells us he wishes to see us again once we are sufficiently rested. The woman leads us to another building, which seems to be a soldier's rest room. We are taken to the washroom, where we remove our clothes and bathe ourselves thoroughly. A bath —what a wonderful treat! The woman brings us clean clothing. She takes the clothes we have been wearing, washes them, and puts them up to dry. Then she shows us to a room where there is a bed—with a real mattress! We fling ourselves upon it. When she returns two minutes later with coffee and food, she has to shake us to get us to sit up and eat. Then she sits down near us and tells us that she used to teach French in Zoliborz, but when the insurrection broke out she joined the Resistance fighters. We tell her of our life in prison. She interrupts us.

"I know all about Auschwitz. I have a son there." Her voice breaks. "I know the Warsaw Ghetto too. . . . Now go to sleep."

She wakes us hours later when the battle around Zoliborz is almost at an end. The Germans are no longer bothering to bomb the district; the last spark of revolt is about to go out. The insurgent troops in Zoliborz have not yet given up the fighting; even though Bor-Komorowski has capitulated, they still hold on. But their loudspeakers are already parleying with the Germans over surrender conditions.

Daniel and I are taken to the commanding officer's room. There we meet the friendly officer. Without any preliminaries, he tells us: "You were wrong to come here. I understand you very well and can imagine that down in the bunker conditions are dreadful, but here we are at the end of our struggle. Perhaps we can still hold out a day or two. But what will you do then?" He speaks bitterly. It is obvious he is an honest man, a true patriot, a sworn enemy of the Germans. He is suffering visibly from defeat, from overwhelming anguish at the sight of so much destruction.

"All the time we hoped some help would come," he continues. "We hoped the Russians would start an offensive. Now we realize this is not yet possible. One of our Polish brigades that is fighting alongside the Russians tried to cross the Vistula near here. Except for a few who managed to escape, it was completely wiped out. Last night, arms were dropped to us by parachute; the Germans intercepted everything." He starts walking agitatedly up and down the room. "We shall be forced to surrender! We have nothing left, neither weapons nor supplies. Our people must not die for nothing."

He stops, is thoughtful for a moment, then comes up to us.

"What do you hope to do now?" Then, without waiting for our reply, he adds: "I advise you to go back to your bunker. There you have a chance of survival. Here, if the Germans return, you will have none. Remain with us as long as we hold out and get back your strength—in your present state, you'll be unable to make the journey back. I will tell you when it's time to go back into the canal and return to your bunker."

We spend three days in Zoliborz, eating and sleeping with the insurgents. They treat us like friends, sharing all they have with us. They know the insurrection is nearing its end. Great suffering and unspeakable bitterness permeate their words. It is not the fear of prison or military camps which makes them sound so hopeless; it is defeat. Opinions are divided as to whether it has all been worthwhile.

There are no more big battles, yet each day brings its sinister harvest of dead and wounded, victims of the few exchanges of fire or the occasional bombs which the Germans are still dropping. What we admire most in the insurgents is their fighting spirit. They know that the end is at hand, that defeat is inevitable, that their resistance can no longer influence the outcome of events; yet they burn with the desire to go on fighting. When an officer asks for men to defend a barricade or for any other action, numerous volunteers come forward. Somc of those volunteers believe that they might still be able to break through the encircling German lines and hide in one of the surrounding villages. But most of the soldiers are resigned. Even while fighting, they are awaiting the moment when the Germans will occupy Zoliborz and take them all captive.

For the two of us, this last possibility does not exist; the Germans must not find us here because for Jews there is only death. We must return to our bunker. The bunker! After having seen daylight, after no longer having to suffer from filth, rats, hunger, and thirst—back to the bunker!

But the officer is right. The bunker is our only hope.

At twilight on the third day, we are asked to leave. The officer says good-bye to us. The woman who has looked after us so well and the three soldiers accompany us until we reach the canal.

At the canal entrance our companions give us two parcels of food, some cigarettes, and a flashlight. The woman remains near the opening to light the way for us. She wishes us a safe return.

Throughout the whole of the long, hard journey back, the warm words of this woman are constantly in my mind. It is a long time since anyone has spoken to us so affectionately.

I lose all track of the hours it takes us to go back to the bunker. Ignace, who is on guard duty that night, is the first to hear our steps. As soon as he sees us, he shouts. "They're back!" Even when we are inside the underground passage that leads to the bunker, he is still shouting: "They're back! Chaim and Daniel are back!"

Our comrades' joy when we are once again among them is indescribable. That moment was the happiest of our entire existence underground. We embrace each other warmly. Then we remove our wet clothes. Hannah lights the stove. We open our parcels—gifts from the insurgents. Bread, salami, biscuits, and tobacco. Our companions shower us with questions. Daniel tells them about the way we were received by the insurgents.

"And the bath!" he says enthusiastically. "We had a bath! That was the best thing of all!

Nothing as wonderful as that has happened to me for years!"

Haskel, who is sitting next to Daniel, groans loudly. "You had a bath, and down here we haven't got even a drop of drinking water!" Daniel and I learn that the spring has dried up.

Isaac rolls a cigarette with the tobacco we have brought, then lights it with the help of a glowing ember from our stove. He breathes in the smoke deeply, savoring it, then says sadly: "Our good times are over. Well, too bad. We'll go back to straining water and boiling it. The rats haven't managed to drink it all yet."

eight

As always, the artillery fire overhead tells us it is time to put out the light. I am so tired after my wanderings in the sewers that I immediately fall asleep. I sleep the whole day without even hearing the usual preparations made by my comrades as night falls. Isaac wakes me and Daniel up—not to have us go out looking for food, for he knows we are too exhausted, but so we can help Hannah prepare the meal and strain the water. But I cannot raise my head; it aches terribly. And my body is bent double. So I stay in bed. Hannah and Daniel have to do the work by themselves.

I am a prey to the deepest despondency. I try in vain to take myself in imagination to pleasanter places. But the bunker pervades my thoughts.

I tell myself that it is the very difficulties of our life underground that help us to go on living, to overcome all sorts of obstacles and keep alive our instinct for survival. One day it is food we are short of, another day we have no water; now danger threatens us from the canal, now the menace seems to come from outside in the yard. One day we struggle against rats, another day against flies; we fear bombardments, stray bullets, patrols. But this daily struggle for existence is good in that it keeps us from becoming apathetic, it forces us to employ all our efforts, all our ingenuity, in order to survive. Without these difficulties we might go mad in this dark, stinking, suffocating hole.

Later, this fact is to appear as clear as daylight to me. But for the moment, lying on the ground in our bunker, I am in such a state that the slightest movement represents an almost superhuman effort for me; it is more by instinct that I struggle against apathy and anguish. I try to take myself back to France, to Paris, to the street leading to Bois Street, where I lived before I was deported and where I left my wife and two children. Lying on the ground, I am back in the first months of the German occupation of France. I recall the first anti-Jewish laws, the first camps at Pithiviers and at Neaune-la-Rolande, where I was interned with so many others. How naive we were then! Why did we not make our escape? Through what stupid optimism did we neglect to go into hiding? But who would have believed then that they would murder women, children, young and old alike in cold blood? Had we not been so childishly hopeful, we could all have made our escape. The people of France would have helped us. How much suffering would we have been spared!

I toss and turn on the hard ground. There is a loud hammering in my head. Pictures of my life in France suddenly disappear, giving way to visions that I am unable to drive away.

June 1942—the road to Auschwitz—jammed

into cattle trucks. Three days without air, without food, squashed together in an atmosphere made foul by the fetid smell of human excrement. But even then not one of us imagined that we were all being taken to our deaths. . . .

I feel as though I cannot breathe. I cry out. Hannah and Daniel rush over to me. Hannah feels my forehead. "He's burning!" she says to Daniel.

She covers me with some old clothes and I fall asleep again. This time, I sleep more peacefully. I am very fortunate. After a day's rest, I am once more on my feet.

The news that Isaac and Ignace begin to bring back from their nightly foraging expedition is far from reassuring. From certain indications they have concluded that other people have been searching through these cellars and yards during the day. These people are certainly not refugees like us, otherwise they would never have dared to come out in the daylight. Our comrades have also concluded from the look of certain cellars that the people who have been searching there are not only interested in food, but also in less perishable objects. In one of the basements all of the wires and electric cables were cut; and in an abandoned yard there was furniture and metalwork carefully packed up as though ready to be transported.

We assume from this that the Germans have been sending civilians into these ruins to collect objects of any value whatever in order to ship it all to Germany. The Germans are not short of slave labor with which to carry out their plans.

And so from this day on, the possibility of obtaining further supplies of food seems much more remote; the people searching the cellars will take away everything. What is worse, in the course of their systematic searching they could come across the pile of debris under which our bunker is situated.

The noise of battle above our heads has become different since our return. The fighting is much less fierce. We believe the two armies are getting ready for a major offensive.

I have a cold and it is difficult for me to breathe in the foul-smelling bunker. That is why, as soon as night falls, I go up to the exit for a bit of fresh air. All around, darkness reigns and a calm which seems like the silence of the grave. Suddenly sounds reach me from the direction of Praga, where the Russian Army is located. I think I am mistaken. Music—here? But soon I can hear again, and much more clearly, the sounds of a mouth organ. I imagine soldiers of the Red Army dancing to the music. I am suddenly seized with an overwhelming hunger for freedom. I want so much to be with other men, to be like them. My heart aches, the music burns my temples! I am even more wretched than before. I put my hands to my ears and go down into the bunker.

Our suspicions about the systematic searching of the cellars are confirmed. Every day people come and work in the ruins. They go down into the basements and take everything out of them. More than once we come back from our expeditions empty-handed. And if ever we do find something, it is scarcely edible, a little food mixed with earth. Just the same, we bring it back to the bunker.

One night, after searching numerous cellars, Ignace brings back a sack half full of oats. He is delighted with it, although it is only with great difficulty that he drags this heavy bag along.

Isaac goes up to this find, inspects it, then exclaims: "What have you brought here, Ignace? That's only good for horses!"

Ignace looks at him and replies very seriously: "And what are we—lions? We're even less than horses!" Then he adds: "When we've nothing else, we will probably find it very appetizing."

For the moment the lack of water is our major concern. We decide that for the next few nights we will not go exploring for food in the cellars. Instead, we will examine the canal to try and find some water.

As soon as night falls, Ignace and Isaac go down into the canal and make their way to the right, while Samek and Haskel go to the left. They return empty-handed.

On the third night Daniel and Isaac are a kilometer from the bunker when they suddenly notice that, in a spot where the canals cross, water is trickling down a wall. This time the water does not fall in drops as it did in our earlier spring, but flows in a steady, slender thread to form a tiny stream.

To reach this new spring, we are forced to pass beneath one of the sewer outlets, covered by a lid, near which is posted a German sentry whose footsteps we can hear. On more than one occasion the Germans have flung gas bombs into these sewer mouths. In spite of this danger, we do not give up our water-gathering expeditions. Indeed, now we have more water than we could ever have obtained from our first spring. We even have enough for washing purposes.

For some days, life is calm in the bunker. We sleep all day and set off in search of food at night. We are constantly forced to widen our circle of exploration, for all the nearby cellars are now empty. Not only is there no food to be found there, but there is no more wood or coal either. Our expeditions last for hours. Each of us invariably manages to unearth something, which he immediately brings back to the bunker.

We do not allow our priest, as we call Kazik, to take part in these expeditions. He is not yet quite well. He coughs much less frequently but he still suffers from intestinal pains, which from time to time become severe cramps.

We have lost all the illusions we once had of the imminence of the Soviet offensive. The Germans are constantly reinforcing their positions along the Vistula. We realize that we cannot live from day to day any longer, and we try to lay in stocks of food for later on. We cannot allow ourselves to let a single night go by without making our searches.

So economy becomes the order of the day: to economize even on the little we have at our disposal, to leave something every day for the following day. We begin to cut down on our rations.

Ignace grumbles: "What's the good of going hungry today when I don't know if I'll still be alive tomorrow."

Each of us harbors thoughts like this. Yet in the bunker there is an unwritten law: we absolutely must cling to the idea that we have a future.

One day there is a particularly fierce bombardment. Shells and bombs explode frequently in the vicinity of our bunker; we are certain we will be blown to pieces.

As soon as calm is restored, a presentiment of an early liberation takes hold of us. This liberation seems so close, we feel we can almost touch it with our fingers; and once more we feel connected to the world of the living.

Several days pass uneventfully. The atmosphere in the bunker is gay again. We tease Hannah, who after completing her household tasks has begun to spend time improving her appearance. She looks at herself in a little mirror and arranges her hair with great care. Daniel regards her lovingly. Samek gazes into her eyes and jokingly asks what "show" she would like to go to that evening.

It is at such moments that we no longer feel like outcasts, like dogs holed up in a bunker, but like members of one family who have freely chosen this communal life.

One thing now begins to concern us: Kazik is complaining more and more of internal pains. One evening as we are getting ready to go out foraging, Kazik does not get up. He covers himself with his coat and groans loudly. We are all very frightened by this. Hannah reassures us, saying she will look after Kazik and make him a hot drink. Isaac puts his hand on Kazik's forehead.

"He has a high temperature," he tells us, adding in a whisper: "It may be typhus."

"I'll stay with Hannah," Ignace declares in Yiddish. "I don't like her going near him when he's this sick."

Some hours later, when we come back to the bunker, we find that Kazik is deathly ill. He is groaning loudly and has terrible internal pains; his fever is steadily rising.

Isaac goes over to him, examines his eyes, takes his pulse, feels his abdomen. Standing around Isaac, we await his diagnosis with great anguish, expecting the worst. Isaac looks at us and says nothing. He sits down and hangs his head. I ask him: "Is it typhus?" He nods.

In the ensuing silence, our eyes fix on the priest, who is twisted with pain. Each of us is thinking: Tomorrow, or the next day, I shall be moaning as he is, I shall suffer as horribly as he is before I die. For how is it possible to avoid catching this disease, living as we do in such close proximity to one another?

Kazik half opens his eyes. "Forgive me. . . ." His voice is full of pleading. "What could I do? I wanted to live. . . ." He gestures vaguely with his hand. Then he closes his eyes and turns his head away.

Now we have a completely unforeseen threat hanging over us, filling the bunker with dread and hopelessness. When day comes, we put out the light and lie down. But none of us can sleep.

I try to think how we can get out of this predicament. There is only one way out: to expedite Kazik's death and throw his body in the canal.

I am convinced this thought has already occurred to all of us but we are unable to say it. Every one of us no doubt sincerely believes that we could easily justify such an act. Millions of Jews have been murdered; Europe is soaked with Jewish blood. Did this priest of ours help to save even one Jewish life? Perhaps there are no more Jews left. Perhaps the Nazis have succeeded in wiping out all the Jews in the countries they have occupied and there will be no one left to bear witness to the horrors of Hitlerism. Who knows if this is not our mission? Should we allow ourselves to perish because of Kazik?

But a feeling of pity stirs in me. I know that the priest is in no way to blame for what has happened. During the insurrection, he fought against our common enemy, even though he fought not for us but for his native land, like a true Polish patriot. Kazik fought the Germans; that should be enough for us.

And conscience also has a word to say. But conscience is stronger—it does not beg; it does not fall at your feet in an attempt to arouse your compassion. On the contrary, it commands. It destroys all your arguments; it shows you that fundamentally you are not concerned about a mission or about benefiting your own people in any way. You are simply afraid for your own life! You want to save it even at the expense of the life of your neighbor. Your conscience rears up before you with a threat: "I shall pursue you for the rest of your life. You will never be free of me. I shall follow you everywhere and harass you to the end of your days!"

I bury my head in my rags and try to think of somcthing else; all to no purposc. I want to stand up and shout; but I cannot. If only the artillery would stop, so we could get up!

We light the lamp and sit in silence. When Hannah starts making a camomile infusion for our invalid, Isaac says to her: "Wait a moment. We must have a discussion."

He speaks in a whisper, in Yiddish, so Kazik will not understand. "It's a hundred-to-one chance," he tells us, "—perhaps the odds are even greater than that—that we will all catch this disease."

"What should we do?" I ask him.

"After thinking about it all night, you ask me this question? I heard you all tossing and turning. You haven't slept, and neither have I. So let's not play with words. It's hard to say it aloud, but we are not children. The danger threatening us is very real. I know we are decent people. But ought we to sacrifice ourselves? Ought we to run such a risk? It will not save him. He cannot hold out."

Isaac is silent. After a moment in which no one has spoken, he speaks again, this time with a note of anger in his voice.

"Do you think I am different from any of you? I suffer even to think of it. But I have to voice my thoughts."

Isaac is right. Faced with the fear that this terrible illness arouses in us, Kazik seems a real enemy against whom we must defend ourselves. We can see only one way out: his swift death! But none of us feels capable of bringing this about. Each time Kazik groans, our hearts ache for him. And when Hannah gets up to heat a little water for him, we are all rather pleased.

To try to change our minds, Hannah says, as though giving voice to silent hope: "Who knows? Perhaps he will get better. Everything is possible."

"You too? You believe in miracles?" Isaac asks her, trying to smile.

"No, but in the times we live in so many things happen which are contrary to all logic and reason, contrary even to medical fact. . . ."

She prepares the infusion. Ignace takes it to the priest. Kazik opens his eyes and smiles. We guess that he is happy to see someone watching over him. His smile expresses all his gratitude.

We look at each other, and—how strange!—it seems to us the situation is no longer the same. We forget the thoughts which tortured us the night before and are happy to think that we have not done anything for which our consciences might later reproach us. We all watch the priest, who lifts the dish to his mouth with both hands. His hands are trembling. Each of us makes the same wish in his heart: may he recover as quickly as possible! And indeed a great surprise awaits us; after drinking the infusion, the priest sits up. He seems to want to say something but is unable to.

"You mustn't talk," Ignace says. "Later, when you are better, you will say all you want to."

Kazik smiles again, but this time his smile is somewhat sarcastic. His face goes red, and he lies back on the ground. "Oh yes, I shall get well. Yes, I shall recover!" His voice is bitter. "Never again shall I enjoy good health. You're all going to see to it that I die as quickly as possible."

"What are you trying to say, Kazik?" Ignace asks.

"What am I trying to say?" He closes his eyes. "Listen, this may be the last time I ever talk to you. But I want you to know that I do not hold it against you. No, no, let me finish. I do not blame you in the least. It is natural that you should think of your own security. You are all good people. You have made me welcome among you." Visibly, he gathers all his strength to raise his voice. "No, you must not die because of me!" Then, after a moment's silence: "But I want to live. I do not want to die. I would so much like to go on living. All of us are right; you must not die; nor must I. As long as I can, I shall cling to life!"

He closes his eyes; big drops of sweat cover his face. We sit there for several minutes without saying anything. None of us seems to know what to say.

Hannah is the first to speak: "Kazik, can't you see that we want to save you?"

But Kazik keeps his eyes closed and makes no reply. He is convinced that we want him to die as quickly as possible. He pulls his coat around him and breathes with difficulty.

We prepare for our foraging expedition. Daniel remembers seeing a cellar full of bottles of all shapes and sizes in the course of one of our expeditions. It was the cellar of a house where a druggist had formerly lived. During the insurrection, the druggist probably hid all these bottles in his cellar. Isaac, who serves as our doctor, thinks that the bottles might contain medicines.

"Come with me," he says to Daniel. "I want you to look for the cellar with the bottles in it.

We might find something to cure our priest."

They set off first, followed by the others, who, as usual, go hunting for food. I stay behind with Hannah.

We are talking quietly together when there is a sudden loud cry. "Oh, dear Jesus, merciful Jesus!" The priest has an extremely painful cramp. We take fright. At once Hannah starts heating some water.

Daniel and Isaac reappear in the bunker. They do not have the medicines for Kazik. They go up to him and look at him, embarrassed, as though they feel guilty.

Isaac declares: "We were very close to that cellar. But a German patrol came toward us, so we ran into one of the ruined houses and managed to slip down into a neighboring cellar and make our way back. But don't worry," he adds, addressing the priest. "We'll go back there again tomorrow."

Isaac smiles to reassure Kazik and then takes his pulse. Hannah and Ignace are seeing to it that there is always hot water. Strange as it may seem after our recent discussions, we are now lavishing all our care on Kazik. No one thinks any longer of the danger of catching his disease.

The following night Daniel and Isaac go off again, looking for medicines. This time they have no difficulty reaching the place they seek.

Back at the bunker again, Isaac shows us a whole parcel of medicines; some can be used for Kazik.

"With these," he says, "you can cure a horse!"

They have found a syringe too. Isaac goes up to our invalid and gleefully shows him the drugs for injection. When the priest sees them, he moans loudly and starts weeping.

"Don't use that," he says with a sob. "I want to die a natural death, not to be killed!" He turns toward the wall.

Despite all the care we have shown him, particularly during the past two days since his illness has got suddenly worse, we have not succeeded in convincing him that we want most sincerely to cure him. No doubt he still thinks that Jews are not to be trusted.

Isaac, still holding the drugs and medicines, looks like someone upon whom cold water has been poured. His face takes on an angry expression.

Immediately Hannah intervenes: "He is ill. He doesn't know what he is saying." She takes the syringe and drugs from Isaac, to get them ready for use. "We'll give him an injection whether he wants it or not. If necessary, we shall have to hold him still."

Ignace leans over the sick man and speaks to him kindly: "Kazik, do you still not trust us?

Don't you believe that we want to help you?" Then he adds: "If we had wanted to kill you, we could have done it a long time ago. We don't need injections for that. Listen, Isaac and Daniel have risked their lives to get medicines and drugs for you. Whether you agree or not, we're going to give you these injections, even if we have to tie you down."

Tears now flow from the sick man's eyes. He crosses himself and starts praying.

When Isaac goes up to him with the syringe, Kazik turns to the wall and holds out an arm. He is trembling with terror.

The next day, after the second injection, our invalid already has a smiling face. He feels a little better.

During the first few days he still hangs his head, as though ashamed at having mistrusted us. Over and over again he repeats: "In your place, others would have acted as I suspected that you might." We understand that in this way he is trying to justify his previous attitude. His return to health gives us the greatest satisfaction and brings us true joy. His recovery reminds us that we have succeeded in conquering ourselves, in triumphing, too, over the barbarous times in which we live. The crimes we have witnessed in the course of the last few years have neither corrupted nor degraded us. We know that we have remained ourselves, that our human feelings are intact, that the life of any man, whoever he may be, is more precious than anything in the world, and that it is our duty to help men to live instead of bringing about their death.

nine

The days drag by slowly. Winter is coming. In the cellars, food supplies are becoming scarcer. We know that as soon as the first snow falls it will be impossible to go out, for our footprints will betray us. That is why we cannot let a single night go by without trying to provide ourselves with stocks of food, wood, and coal.

Kazik is getting better with each day that passes, and like all convalescents he needs something substantial to eat. He would very much like to take part in our expeditions, but we do not allow him to do this yet because they are becoming more and more exhausting and complicated. We are forced to travel long distances and to search in the ruins for hours on end before we find anything at all. And always there is the threat of being caught by German patrols, which are on the move all over the ruined city. More than once, sentries who have heard our footsteps have opened fire, and we have had to abandon our find in order to make our escape through the cellars.

But all this does not discourage us. Our nightly sorties are of vital importance. We now know absolutely by heart the underground routes for several miles around; we recognize every stone. We have even drawn up signs which enable us to recognize things in the dark. We continue our operations in pairs, so as to be able to explore several places during the course of a single night.

Hannah and the priest remain in the bunker and take care of the cooking. Our Hannah excels in her scrupulously fair division of our food. She uses a cup as a measure and each one of us gets an exact share. Each of us is entitled to a plate of soup, and if there is any left it is divided equally. When we have potatoes, Hannah does detailed calculations to allocate so much per head. This meticulous sharing is indispensable in the life we lead. It also avoids useless, even dangerous, arguments.

Our nerves are strained. The best times for us are when we return to the bunker and sit down at the table. Then we are often even gay, because we are safely back together. The bunker seems transformed, pervaded by a family atmosphere. Each of us relates the details of his expedition. We even tease Ignace, who is very timid. Indeed, each time he comes back, he is tense and for a long time incapable of moving.

Tension always precedes the return of the foragers. The time which elapses between the separate arrival of the three pairs of explorers is particularly painful, for it is impossible to calculate the exact duration of each search. When one group comes back, we wait impatiently for the second. It is when this group comes that

Hannah sets the table. Then we await the return of the third group.

That is the hardest time. Each minute seems an eternity. We imagine that terrible things are happening to our companions. The smell of the soup tickles our nostrils and increases our impatience; but until everyone is back in the bunker, we do not sit down at the table. This is one of our unwritten laws.

Only once do we transgress this law. We are awaiting the return of Daniel and Isaac, the last pair. Hannah sets the table as usual, gaily announcing a surprise: on hot bricks she has cooked for each of us a kind of small flat cake. "But," she says to us, "don't chew it too much, because the flour is mixed with sand." So there we are, awaiting the fine dinner in store for us. But Daniel and Isaac are still not back. An hour passes. We tell ourselves they must have gone a long way from the bunker and it is taking them longer than usual to find their way back.

After hours of waiting, we cannot help thinking that something has gone wrong. The artillery overhead tells us it is day; still no Daniel, no Isaac. Now we are almost certain that they have been shot or captured. The fire on which our dinner is simmering begins to go out, but no one seems to notice. The smell of the soup fades away completely. We forget our hunger. Hannah insists on keeping her head down, lest we see her tear-filled eyes. No one even considers that their misfortune could bring similar misfortune upon us: we are absolutely certain that they would never betray us.

Our priest Kazik begins to pray. Haskel mutters between his teeth: "He's a hothead, that Isaac. He's gone rushing into some danger and has dragged Daniel with him."

Ignace explodes: "What do you think he ought to do—sit on the floor and groan like you? If it weren't for Isaac we would have had nothing to eat for a long time now!"

Isaac never spares himself. He does not hesitate to explore the remotest cellars. And on nights when for some reason or other we are forced to abandon the idea of a foraging party, he is incapable of sitting still.

The day is advanced. We sit at the table and have something to eat, and then we lie down. But we cannot sleep. The two empty places stare at us in the darkness. Where are they?

Samek, lying near me, cannot sleep either. He asks me in a whisper: "What do you think, Chaim? Do you think they'll come back? Maybe they've holed up in some cellar or other, waiting for nightfall."

None of us wants to resign himself to the possibility that after suffering so much, after going through so much, he might die at the very last moment in the ruins of Warsaw. All of us are wide awake now, suffering from their absence as if one of our limbs had been amputated.

The day drags along endlessly. When night finally comes, we decide to give up our foraging expedition this time: Isaac and Daniel might have been caught near our bunker, in which case the Germans will have left sentries on the spot. To go out might mean the end of us all. So I go with Haskel into the canal to get water. Samek is on guard at the canal entrance. Nervously, Hannah wanders around the bunker, forgetting to prepare food. Ignace takes our "lavatory" basin down to the canal. When we return to the bunker, Isaac and Daniel are still not back. A dreadful foreboding grips us all. We tell ourselves there is no hope.

Several hours go by. Suddenly, Samek, who is standing guard near the opening, shouts: "They're here!"

The next moment, he joins us. Isaac and Daniel are behind him. They look exhausted. All of us embrace them. Hannah is filled with joy. She immediately sets to work. Haskel helps her.

"You were not expecting us back anymore, were you?" Daniel says, and he looks at Hannah to see the expression on her face. Their eyes meet.

Isaac interrupts this somewhat embarrassing exchange. "You think we didn't realize what you must have been feeling?" he says. "There was nothing we could do about it. We had rotten luck right from the beginning. We couldn't find a thing. Finally, we crossed a street and went in a house. In the basement were some dried kidney beans, and in another cellar we found some oats. When we went into the last cellar of that house, we lit our candle to see if there was anything interesting there. But a German sentry was posted near the cellar grating, and he spotted the light. Immediately he cried: 'Who goes there?' I blew out the candle quickly and stayed there, motionless, holding my breath. But the German shouted a second time: 'Who's there? Come out!' Then he fired in the air to call other sentries to his aid.

"We thought we were through. We'd be dead now if we had stayed a minute longer in that cellar. But as he fired, the German came up to the entrance to the part of the cellar that was a long way from the grating. Without wasting a moment, we left the basement and reached the yard. Bullets whistled above our heads. We went straight into the second house and from there into the third.

"Meanwhile the firing had intensified. Our German was not the only one shooting at us. Just the same, we went on running from cellar to cellar without knowing where we were going. In the end we managed to give the Germans the slip. Then we had to rest awhile; we were worn out. And when we were ready to come back to the bunker, we saw it was almost day. It was too late. So we went down into the cellar of a demolished house and lay beneath a pile of debris the whole day. And finally—here we are!"

There is no expedition that night. For us it is a celebration. And when at last we taste the meager soup and the sandy bread cakes, they have an indescribably delicious flavor.

It may very well be that these rare moments of joy give us the strength to carry on our struggle for survival.

Life in the bunker continues at a standstill. The hours stretch out endlessly. During the day we lie around in silence. At night we forage. Except for these foraging expeditions, there is not much to do. We have already told each other all we have to tell. It often happens that we spend whole hours now without exchanging a word. Each of us is deep in his own thoughts.

You might think that such an existence would gradually become a sort of lethargic half-sleep. But the truth is that lack of conversation is only one aspect of our life underground. We still have to struggle day and night for our existence. I often tell myself that such a struggle is more difficult than open combat. Not only do we have to confront several enemies at once but also we are forced to combat something invisible, unknown, unforeseeable. We never know from what direction death threatens, but we know perfectly well that it lies in wait for us all the time. It could come from the outside or from the canal, from hunger or thirst, from something altogether unforeseen. These fears torment us.

With the coming of winter the flies have disappeared. But now we have another scourge—rats. Each day they become more and more numerous. They are large creatures, and they come in packs from the canal and from the hole which leads outside. Perhaps they can no longer find corpses to devour in the ruins; or they may have been driven out by the German soldiers who are now standing guard in the cellars. The fact that these rats only invade our bunker by day, when we are sleeping, confirms the second supposition. It is true that there have always been rats in the canal, but in the beginning our presence seemed to frighten them and they withdrew and left us alone. We could only hear their screeching. Now, maddened by the German guards, they are taking refuge with us. Besides, it is probably warmer here.

Ignace is the first to cry out in alarm. All of a sudden he wakes us in the middle of the night, and starts shouting. We jump up, terrified, fearing our hiding place has been discovered.

"What is it, Ignace?"

"The rats bit me!" he groans, feeling at his body. At first we think that he has been dreaming. But he insists that several rats attacked and bit him—and this turns out to be true. From then on Ignace does not lie down until he has armed himself with a stick.

Finally, we succeed in solving this problem as best we can: we decide that the one who is on guard after the meal must also see to it that the rats do not enter the bunker and attack us.

Our struggles with ourselves are as arduous as those with the rats—but in a different way. We struggle so as not to let ourselves be overcome by apathy and resignation. Often after our meal, which takes place at about three o'clock in the morning, a great fit of depression overwhelms us and no one is able to say a word.

Haskel is most subject to these fits of depression. Sitting on the ground, he puts his elbows on his knees, his head in his hands, and remains like this for a long time, without making the slightest movement. When Daniel is depressed, he usually lies face down, leans his head on his hands, and looks fixedly at the ground without saying a word. Is he weeping? No one dares look at him in these moments of sadness. When Hannah and Samek have a fit of black depression, they remain seated close to each other, yet they seem to be separated by thousands of miles. And when Isaac is depressed, he goes off toward the canal entrance and watches the filthy waters flow by.

Kazik, like the good priest he is, gets out his prayer book and loses himself in a prayer as soon as he becomes aware of our depression. If an attack were to be launched against us at a moment like this, we wouldn't even notice it; we would be captured in these different positions. At such times we are all far away from the bunker, carried off into the past to our former homes, to the lives we lived before the war.

Occasionally, when I somehow manage to break away from this bleak atmosphere, I scrutinize my comrades. It would be thoughtless and agonizing for me to disturb this escape of theirs; let them dream like this for an hour or two more; we need our dreams. In any case, the artillery will soon announce a new day and will bring them back to the reality of the bunker. So I never disturb them. Instead, I climb toward the bunker entrance, shift the bricks which cover it, and look out at the ruins of Warsaw lying all around us. Often I recall the day I returned to Warsaw together with two thousand other deported Jews to clean up the ruins of the ghetto. . . .

On the night of October 1943, at Auschwitz-

Birkenau, an alarm was sounded, followed by the brutal order: "Outside! Roll call!" Such alarms usually boded no good and each of us expected the worst. We thought it meant a new selection for the gas chambers. Ten days earlier, such a selection cost the lives of fifteen hundred deportees. My closest friends from Paris were among the victims.

But this selection was for another purpose. A thousand men were selected, I among them. We were sent from Birkenau to Auschwitz, where another thousand Jews already awaited us. We were all loaded into cattle cars. After a day's journey the train stopped. Through tiny windows with thick bars, we could see a few twinkling lights against a dark background. Later, when we were ordered to get down, the sky was already light.

Immediately, the SS surrounded us on all sides. Their commanding officer told us that we were in Warsaw to do a certain job. "If you work well, you will live!"

Warsaw! The name had a shattering effect upon me. This was the city where I was born, where I grew up, where my family lived, and where they probably all perished. I knew that all the Jews of Warsaw had been exterminated. Warsaw! The city of the ghetto uprising, whose echoes reached even our camp and filled us all with pride, with sadness, with hope. How we had reacted in camp to the news of the heroic fighting in Warsaw!

The place where we stood—as we discovered later—was the sadly famous Umschlagplatz. From here the Jews of the Warsaw Ghetto had been taken to the gas chambers of Treblinka.

Later, we were marched through Pokorna Street, Muranowski Square, Mila Street, and Zamenhof Street (formally called Dzika Street) to Gesia Street. We stopped near the military prison.

Five months had gone by since the end of the ghetto revolt. All around us now there was nothing but destruction and ruins, not a living soul. Here and there lay abandoned objects, mute witnesses of a human past: torn books, pages from the Talmud, misshapen beds, fragments of scrolls of the Law. A landscape of death.

The ruins inspired in us a sense of awe: we were the first to tread the sacred soil of the ghetto!

When we reached the yard of the military prison, where a camp had been prepared for us, we found about fifty young Jews there. They were locked up in our cells. Every day at dawn military trucks came and took them away; every evening they were brought back. Rumor had it that the Germans had rooted them out of sewers and bunkers. Soon after our arrival they were all shot.

I was assigned to a group of about ten men. Our work consisted of exploring cellars and ruins in the ghetto to gather up all electrical materials—wires, transformers, and the like.

Two SS men guarded us. Usually they stayed outside while we searched the cellars for objects which could be used in electrical installations. These objects would later be sent to Germany.

One day in the course of our searchings I went down into a cellar on Dzielna Street, if I am not mistaken, with a comrade named Solomon (who was to fall in the ranks of the Warsaw insurgents in August). In one of the walls of this cellar we discovered a hole. We went through it into a second cellar, from which a door led to a third. We made our way into it and stood rooted to the spot with surprise. That cellar was completely full of books. They were not just odd volumes scattered about or hastily flung on the ground. All these books were carefully arranged in rows. We had the impression that entire libraries had been taken down there. We thumbed through a few volumes and realized that nearly all the books were in Yiddish. This discovery overwhelmed us; it was like a call from another universe which had disappeared long ago. Forgetting where we were, forgetting too that the SS were waiting for us outside, we went on thumbing through the books.

Another opening took us to a sort of alcove stacked with volumes of the Talmud. Some of them were yellow with age and worn with use.

We knew we had to leave that cellar; each minute's delay would cost us dearly; we would be beaten, whipped. But we stood as though riveted to this enchanted place. We pulled out a book here, another there. I had the feeling that a whole world was throbbing between my fingers.

"Solomon," I said to my comrade. "What about taking a few books back to camp?"

Without any hesitation, he replied: "You are right. Look, here are the works of Sholem Aleichem."

We each took a few volumes, pulled off the covers, undid the lining of our trousers, and slipped the pages inside. Then we left the cellar. One of the SS guards shouted obscenities at us. But that was all.

That evening as we went into the camp, Solomon and I kept very close to each other. This was the usual procedure when we had an object hidden on us, for if the SS who were checking the prisoners found some object on the first one, his attention would then be focused on him and the second prisoner could more easily slip into the camp.

But the magic of Sholem Aleichem worked wonders: we were searched without incident.

That night, when the SS left the camp and when, in their turn, the guard and the camp supervisor withdrew, we called our comrades together in a corner, and in a low voice I read them a story by Sholem Aleichem. Which one? I don't remember anymore. But what I do remember very well is the sight of those faces made gay by his humor, the stifled laughter (for we were forbidden to laugh) of all those Jews condemned to death who forgot for a while where they were and what awaited them.

Before lying down, I hid the two books under a plank in the ceiling of our barracks. All during those long weeks of labor, Sholem Aleichem brought us great joy and consolation.

Everywhere in the Jewish quarter we found traces of fighting. Cleaning out a house in Nalewki Street near Krasinski Park, I discovered some Jewish corpses in a shop. They had been suffocated; they lay beneath a mass of debris. They were no doubt combatants in the ghetto. In a yard in Swietojerska Street, we found numerous remains of bearded Jews, probably Chasidim. Indeed, I was to learn later that there had once been a brush factory on that spot which had employed a large number of pious Jews, who had fought valiantly. In the cellars too we often stumbled upon the bodies of those who had fought in the ghetto.

When we arrived in Warsaw, we noticed that cucumbers were growing in numerous courtyards in the ghetto. Some of those yards were not too badly destroyed. Though littered with masonry they resembled meadows, for they were entirely covered with leaves, among which cucumbers were to be found. This was an inexplicable thing for us. But at the sight of those appetizing vegetables, we hardly bothered to ask questions. We literally flung ourselves upon them. More than one of us owed our lives to these providential little cucumbers. They made me think of the manna in the Bible—their taste seemed so sweet to me!

After gathering up all the electrical materials, our procedure was to demolish the walls of burnt-out houses which still remained standing in the ghetto. One day, carrying picks and shovels, we went into the yard of one of these houses. I noticed that this square was covered with cucumber leaves. Making certain that the guard could not see me, I set to work; with one hand I pulled the leaves aside, with the other I picked the cucumbers, which I munched on the spot.

All of a sudden, I saw a human eye fixed on me from beneath the foliage! The blood congealed in my veins, a piece of cucumber stuck in my throat, and I literally felt my hair stand on end. A second later, when I got my wits back, I realized that a dead Jew lay on his back among the leaves, his body curled up, his arms crossed; the man was probably trying to protect himself in this way from the cold. A few leaves had stuck to his long beard; near him I noticed the round black hat worn by pious Jews. He seemed to have been dead two or three days. Perhaps he had lived here among the ruins for many months before succumbing to the cold and to hunger.

I felt ill, as though I was about to faint. I gathered my last strength to get up, but once on my feet I let out a wild cry. My comrades came running up to me. We all stood petrified around the dead man.

The shouting of the SS and the guard, and the blows which began to rain down upon us, brought us back to reality.

Only once did we discover a living being—a young girl. In Wolynska Street, a platoon of us Jews guarded by an SS man went down into a cellar which led into another cellar. In the second cellar we suddenly saw a young girl, who looked to us like something wild and prehistoric. Near her lay the body of a young man.

The Germans ordered us to take the corpse outside. They took the girl off to the camp. There they got her to calm down and to wash herself; they also gave her something to eat.

When we came back to the camp at lunchtime we were all ordered to remain standing. The girl was sitting on a chair near the kitchen.

The commandant went up to her and said: "Here, in this camp, Jews live. No harm is done to them. They work and they are fed. You too can stay here and live. You will go short of nothing. You only have to tell us who helped you to survive until now. With whom are you in contact? With someone outside? Tell me, child."

The girl looked at him with an expression of pride. There was a light on her face, as though she was glowing from within. She leaped up from her chair and said with contempt in her voice:

"I know your sweet words! But you will pay for everything! Your end is already near!"

The commandant shot her through the heart.

The noise of falling bricks and rubble brings me back from my memories. At first I think it is another trick the rats are playing on us, but as I strain my ears I can make out the sounds of several people walking nearby.

Abruptly they stop, as though looking for something. I realize that these are not Germans. It is not at all their characteristic booted tread. I am convinced that these are refugees living in the sewers; like us they are trying to find food in the ruins of Warsaw.

Quietly I crawl in their direction so as to be able to hear their voices. I hear nothing but the noise of their receding footsteps. A moment later there is total silence.

I race back and go tumbling down into the bunker, frightening everyone. My companions think that I am being pursued.

"What is happening?" Hannah exclaims.

"I heard footsteps in the yard!"

"What?" says Ignace. "You must have been dreaming. Who can be wandering around in the yard now?"

"I swear it was footsteps. I even went close to make sure."

"Well, what of it?" Ignace asks.

"I heard them going off toward the ruins on the other side of the yard."

Isaac, who cannot contain himself any longer,

turns on Ignace: "Why won't you believe it? It's possible other Jews are hidden in a bunker and are looking for food."

"Why only Jews? It is possible that they are Christians," Samek says. "Many Poles belonging to the Resistance movement told me during the last days of the insurrection that they were ready to do anything to escape being captured by the Germans."

"No," Isaac says heatedly. "It's true that there were members of the Resistance who wanted to hide in the sewers. But now that Poles, directed by the Germans, are working in the ruins, non-Jewish insurgents wouldn't hesitate to contact them, and so they would no longer be in hiding. We alone have to stay in the sewers—because we are Jews!"

"But why suppose?" Hannah intervenes. "It would be more sensible to go and find out who these people are."

We are like men abruptly aroused from a deep sleep. The dark thoughts which absorbed us a few moments ago are already forgotten. All our attention is now concentrated on one single point: who are the people whose footsteps I heard? The possibility that these strangers could be Jews creates a bond between them and us. Each of us tries to remember at what points in the old part of the city there were Jewish Resistance fighters. Isaac recalls seeing some of them in Kozla Street. So we decide that on the following night we will go down into the cellars on the other side of the yard. Perhaps our strangers have set up their bunker over there.

We search for them that night. We find no one.

The next morning artillery fire starts up again with particular violence. We hear aircraft overhead. Such trials of strength between the Soviet Army at Praga and the German Army on this side of the Vistula are frequent. On certain days the firing has been so heavy that it seemed our bunker was being shaken to its foundations. Now planes circle about us, and we have the impression they are passing right over our heads. The throbbing of their engines deafens us. Occasionally these battles have lasted three or four days. Sometimes they go on late into the night and take place not only above us but also in an area covering several miles.

This battle continues for days. Then there is a day of complete silence. Not a single shot is fired during the entire day! We begin to think that the Germans have already left, that the Russians have entered Warsaw without our knowing it.

We live through unbearable hours of tension as we wait for nightfall. From our opening we can see very little because of the pile of debris. In order to see more, we would have to climb very high and lean outside completely, but by day this is too dangerous.

Night arrives. One by one we look outside to see what has happened.

Nothing has changed. Our disappointment is so great that we do not have even the courage to go and search for food.

Such days of waiting and disillusion occur frequently. Each time we think we have distinguished infallible signs which herald our deliverance, they turn out to be mere figments of our imagination. We end by realizing that the artillery duels do not necessarily signify the beginning of the Russian offensive. That this offensive will come one day we do not doubt. But that day will certainly be much later than we imagined. And, gradually, we realize that our stay in the bunker will last a long time.

At the beginning of November a new complication arises in our underground existence. We begin to feel the vicious bite of the cold.

It is especially when we lie down to sleep that we feel the cold. The old rags which serve us as coverings are insufficient. We begin to explore the cellars carefully to try to find materials with which to cover ourselves. We think too of altering our stove so that it can warm the bunker. Of course, it is Haskel whose task it will be to make this transformation.

"I know how to do it. I only need the pipes," he says.

In the ruins there is no shortage of pipes. It is just a matter of collecting them and bringing them to the bunker. So from now on one more task is added to our worries: to overcome the cold. We pile up everything we can lay our hands on: coal, wood, rags, as well as pipes for Haskel.

Haskel allows no one to help him. All on his own, he molds the clay and puts one brick on top of another, with the same precision he would employ if he were installing a stove in his own house. During the days that he devotes to altering the stove, he becomes a different man. His tongue is loosened; he is no longer our usual Haskel. Work makes him forget his misfortunes.

He constructs the stove in such a way that it can be used to cook on as well; he builds it after the style normally used in Polish villages. He erects a wall about three feet high and of approximately the same length; its width is something like eighteen inches. In the middle of the stove he makes two identical holes and separates them with a kind of screen. He makes openings into which coal can be fed. The depth of these openings is also about eighteen inches. The stove is covered with a sheet of tin in which Haskel has cut two holes for cooking; on the side he makes another opening, the width of which corresponds with the length necessary to reach the exit to the bunker.

When the stove is ready, Haskel will let no one light it for the first time. That is his task! His face radiates satisfaction. On one of the holes on the top of the stove Hannah puts our soup to boil: water with a little vermicelli in it and the inevitable grains of sand.

"The hole is, of course, for roasting our meat on!" Hannah says to Haskel. We all laugh. Haskel lights the stove. When he is satisfied that the fire has caught and that the stove does not smoke, he grins broadly.

But Ignace, who is on guard near the entrance, suddenly dives back into the bunker. "Quick, put the fire out!" he shouts.

"What's going on?" Hannah asks him.

"Quick, be quick, put out the fire! Put it out!"

We do as he says. Ignace tells us that the smoke from the stove was drifting toward the German patrols.

"I can fix that," Haskel says, after a moment's reflection.

He lights the fire again, then climbs toward the exit and with the help of a bit of rag disperses the smoke. This way it cannot go very far. We take turns doing this until daybreak; then we put out the fire, remove the end of the pipe which goes through to the other side of the wall, and block up the hole.

Our expeditions are made more difficult by the cold, because we must now bring back to the bunker not only food but something for heat as well. In most of the cellars, the stairs have been either burned or demolished. So we must resort to all sorts of expedients to get down into them and come back up again loaded with fuel. More than once we run the risk of falling back into a cellar and of not being able to get up again, especially in our state of physical weakness. What is more, we are forced to venture farther and farther afield. Such expeditions sometimes take us five or six hours.

One night during a foraging expedition with Isaac, I make my way down into the cellar of one of the destroyed houses—and we detect a noise. It is as though someone is coming and going inside. We are not frightened; we know that the Germans never come down into the cellars at night. It occurs to us that these are the same fugitives whose steps I heard some time ago in the yard above our bunker.

My heart starts beating violently and in a half-choked voice I manage to say in Yiddish: "Who's there?"

There is no reply.

We tell ourselves that perhaps they are Poles. So this time it is Isaac who asks in Polish: "Who's there? We are Jews. Don't be afraid!"

With that we risk going into the cellar. Isaac

strikes a match and by its flickering light we make out two men crouched in a corner, clinging to each other in fear. They are so terrified they cannot utter a single word. Yes, this is how it is; under the ground, we are like animals of the same species who are afraid of each other. I light a candle, and it is only then that they pull themselves together and exclaim joyfully:

"Jews!"

They fling themselves into our arms and burst out sobbing.

We remain like this for some time, our arms around each other, without being able to say a word.

They are about forty years old, but so hairy and so covered with dust that they seem more like sixty. Presumably we look very much the same to them. One of them comes from Belgium; his name is Wasserman. He too was taken from Auschwitz to Warsaw, where he was set free by the insurrection. The second one is called Hurwitz. He hid in the "Aryan" part of Warsaw. Both of them took part in the insurrection, fighting nearby on the banks of the Vistula. They are not alone. There are ten of them, all men, fugitives who have gone into hiding. They have a bunker in Kozla Street. All of them fought in the ranks of the People's Army.

"What about you?" they ask us.

Briefly we tell them our story.

"It is very, very hard," Wasserman complains. "Who knows if we shall manage to hold out with so little food. And now the cold!"

"Where do you find water?"

"We are not at all well off for water. We get ours from the filthy barrels left behind in the yards. You remember those huge barrels filled with water which were placed in each yard during the insurrection to be used for putting out fires? They were to be our water reserves too in case the Germans decided to cut off our water supplies. That's the water we use. But even that is beginning to run short and we have to go looking for water a long way off."

"How is your hiding place disguised? Have you a second exit so you can make your escape if your bunker is discovered?"

"No," Wasserman replies. "Come and see for yourselves."

We set off with them through cellars and ruins and reach a yard surrounded by gutted houses. The whole yard is full of broken bricks and stones. On the right, in the corner, we see the entrance to a ruined house. In front of this entrance is another pile of stones and bricks which the fugitives have heaped up in order to disguise the entrance to their bunker. We scale this and enter a corridor. One side leads to the upper stories by means of a staircase that has been burned almost to ashes. We go along the other side through a hole toward the cellar, which is concealed behind a big pile of bricks, stones, and the remains of metalwork. We see an opening through which a man might squeeze. Near this opening, one of the fugitives is always on guard.

Their cellar consists of two little rooms. The first room is occupied by the one who is on guard. His companions are in the other room. When we arrive Hurwitz says to the guard: "Shalom." Then we go in.

The astonishment of the bunker inhabitants is so great that they are rooted to the spot. To meet Jewish survivors, here, beneath the ruins of Warsaw! They could not even imagine it. For us too this is a fantastic vision from beyond the tomb. They come from different places: from the camp in Gesia Street, for Pawiak Prison, from hiding places in the "Aryan" quarter of the city. All of them were part of the same detachment of the People's Army.

We cannot linger very long with them; it is late and we have to traverse many cellars and ruins in order to reach our own bunker. We take leave of our newfound brothers and promise them that we will soon return.

When we come out, Isaac whispers to me: "Did you see how they looked, Chaim? They're half dead."

"They have lost hope," I reply.

Later, when we return and tell our comrades

that we found some Jews and were with them in their bunker, all of them want to go and see them immediately.

"The other day, when you told us you had heard steps in the yard, I knew they had to be Jews!" Ignace says in a weary voice, as though he is talking to himself.

"Now who except Jews would be hiding in bunkers?"

"What do they look like? Have they any food and water?"

"Tell me," Hannah says. "Have they a sewer where they can take refuge in case of danger?"

"No, they've only a bunker hidden behind a pile of stone and bricks."And briefly I describe to them our new friends' shelter. "As for food, they struggle to get hold of some, just as we do."

"But they can't be left in such a situation!" Hannah exclaims. "What if they are tracked down, what will become of them? Where will they take refuge?"

"And what if *we* are discovered, where shall *we* run to?" Daniel retorts, smiling at her maliciously.

"At least we can hide in the canal," insists Hannah.

"If we are forced to take refuge in the canal, the rats will eat us alive there!" Haskel observes, clipping his words.

Isaac tries to calm Hannah. "They are armed.

They will defend themselves if they are attacked."

"But they will perish!" she cries.

"It really would be a shame to die just now, just when the end is so close," Kazik says, crossing himself.

From that moment a new life begins in the bunker. We are not only concerned for ourselves but also for them—perhaps because they are more vulnerable than we or perhaps simply because they are Jews, miraculously saved from the great butchering. We feel ourselves closely bound to them.

Before the insurrection, in the camp set up on the site of the former Warsaw Ghetto, where Mowolipki Street was situated, rose a church which had remained undamaged. That was the only building left standing in the midst of the ruins, and from far off you could see its steeple. Certain pious Christians considered it a miracle and saw in it the symbol of the superiority of their religion over Judaism. The Germans used that church for their own ends. It was against one of its walls that they found it convenient to shoot Polish Resistance fighters.

Every day, at dawn, Polish patriots were taken there in armored cars to be executed. These cars were escorted by the SS. When they stopped near the church, the platoons of deportees working nearby were forced to move off.

Then the SS made their prisoners get down from the cars, lined them up against the wall of the church, and shot them. We heard the cries of these poor wretches—cries of anguish, but also of courage and dignity in the face of death. "Long live liberty! Long live Poland! Down with Fascism!"

Sometimes the condemned men started singing "The Internationale" or Polish national songs, until they were stopped by a hail of bullets. Our hearts bled for them as if they were our own brothers. Their suffering linked them with us, just as our new comrades in the other bunker are also bound to us now through our common lot.

After each of those executions, I would think of those who had been shot. I would imagine their bearing, their faces. I would try to piece together their lives. Their deaths haunted me.

We are constantly thinking of the ones in the other bunker. Can we perhaps take them into our own bunker, so that we can all be together? We know that this is physically almost impossible; there will be no room to turn around. Yet when Isaac asks us if he can go over to them the following night and suggest that they join us, we all agree.

It is still dark. We continue to talk about the others. The fact that they had fought in the

People's Army reminds us again of the Polish Resistance. We find ourselves talking about the revolt. And once again I am telling them how I obtained my freedom.

"It was a Tuesday, I think, the first of August. The Warsaw camp where I was at the time had been evacuated three days previously. There were four hundred and thirty Jews, and we had to help pack and send off different objects which had been left behind in the camp. In the morning of that day we were lined up ready to set off for our work. The SS were grouped around us, as usual. Suddenly an SS officer arrived and said a few words to the commandant. The latter ordered us to get into groups of five. He stopped at the second row and commanded the new formation to step forward five paces. I was among them.

"There were about fifty of us. The SS told us that we were going to transfer the contents of two depots into wagons. We were taken to what had been the Umschlagplatz. Empty wagons were waiting for us. We began to load them with footwear and other goods.

"The SS were much on edge. They made two rows around us and kept hitting us on the head with the butts of their guns and shouting: 'Quicker, quicker!'

"To avoid these blows we had to run without

stopping. Toward five in the evening, a number of SS officers put in a sudden appearance. They conversed in low voices with their colleagues, whose duty it was to guard us. They seemed frightened. Then they went away as fast as they had come.

"Suddenly we heard shooting. Soon we could see men armed with machine guns running toward us as they fired. I thought a group of partisans had attacked our camp. This happened from time to time. The SS took up positions and began replying to the fire. We were pushed inside a depot and the SS bolted the doors. One of them came in with us and, training his machine gun on us, ordered: 'Lie on the floor and don't move, otherwise I'll fire!'

"We fell to the ground. Some of the prisoners sobbed, others murmured the prayer *Shema Yisroel*, still others recited psalms aloud. Outside, the firing became more and more intense. Inside that depot, we were certain that the SS would machine gun us at any moment.

"Slowly, the firing grew weaker; then it stopped. There was a violent knocking on the door of our depot. A voice shouted in Polish: 'Open up!' Before the SS had time to train his machine gun on the door, it was thrown open and he collapsed, struck dead by a bullet.

" '*Jestescie Wolni*! You are free!'

"These words were uttered by a man about thirty years old, carrying a machine gun and wearing a red and white armband. He was the commander of the detachment which had attacked our depot. We went wild with joy! To describe such a moment is impossible. We ran toward the yard where the partisans—about forty of them—were assembled. We embraced each other. They went and fetched our comrades who had remained behind in the camp. This fraternization had something incomparably beautiful about it. Here were men who could not even understand each other—for the Hungarian Jews among us spoke only their own language and German. What did that matter? We understood each other just the same. We smiled at each other; the expression on our faces said more than all the language in the world. The sight of the corpse of our *Obsenscharfsfuhrer* who, together with his minions, had so cruelly beaten us all day but was now lying there like a dead rat, was for me—I must admit—the pleasantest surprise.

"The partisans had suffered no losses in their ranks except for four wounded. I was so overwhelmed by all these events that the sense of them actually escaped me. I did not yet understand that it was the beginning of the general uprising in Warsaw and I continued to think that it was only one attack, launched by a detachment of partisans, who would soon leave this place to rejoin their comrades. I was ready to follow them.

"While all this was happening, one of our liberators came up and asked which of us spoke Polish. Immediately I stepped forward. He took me to a room. I saw an officer and five other members of the Resistance, one of whom was a doctor. They were sitting around a table covered by a map of Warsaw on which certain points were underlined in red.

"The officer asked me where I came from and in what camps I had been interned. I replied: 'Auschwitz.'

"They looked at each other.

"I added that before leaving for France I had lived in Warsaw. The officer said to me: 'We will call you the man from Warsaw,' and this nickname stuck to me.

"He then informed me that the general insurrection which had been carefully arranged a long time ago by the Polish Home Army had just broken out in Warsaw, and that his group had been entrusted with the task of attacking the point where we were. Another formation had gone into the former ghetto to liberate the camp in Gesia Street. Had they succeeded? He did not yet know.

"The insurgents intended staying there for the night. Patrols were organized. As soon as night fell, one of these patrols had to go to the outlying districts near Gesia Street. Immediately I offered to accompany it because I knew all the ruined ghetto streets which led to the camp. The Resistance fighters happily accepted my proposal. Thereupon the commanding officer asked me to tell the other Jews not to disperse and that they could have whatever there was in the depot. This depot was bursting with bread, biscuits, various canned and bottled objects, among which were thousands of cans of beef.

" 'But advise them to be careful,' said the doctor. 'Obviously they are starving; tell them not to eat too much at once. They can die from overeating. You must tell them that one mouthful too much could cost them their lives.'

"When I left the officer and his companions, I had to search for my comrades for some time; they had already made their way into the different depots. The sensible words of the doctor had no effect on these famished men. After so many years of the most terrible privations, the sight of the loaves of bread and the huge piles of canned meat made the pangs of hunger too much to bear. They threw themselves upon the food, tearing apart the loaves of bread and stuffing the pieces into their mouths. They broke open the cans with their hands and paid no attention to the metal that gashed their fingers and palms;

they did not even see the blood flowing from their hands, they were so busy emptying one can after another. With their torn fingers they fished out the bits of meat and stuffed them in their mouths. No one could have stopped them.

"Later, dysentery did its deadly work. Many of them did not live to see the liberation.

"Toward the end of that day I was sitting on a stone outside the depot. It was twilight and for the first time in many years I breathed the fresh air peacefully, with delight, like a free man. As I thought about the events of that day, I wondered: Am I really free? I still could not believe it. I knew nothing about the politics of the insurrection, but it gave me great joy for it had unleashed a major struggle against the occupying power.

"The commanding officer asked the Jews to assemble.

" 'The insurrection has just broken out,' he said. 'Each of you is free to stay here, if he so wishes. But you can also join us in our fight against the Nazis.'

"With the exception of a few sick men, we all expressed our wish to fight the Germans.

"When it was quite dark, the commanding officer came up to me. There were five soldiers with him, all carrying machine guns which they had made themselves. I was given some hand grenades. It was already dark.

"We left the yard without making any noise. The commanding officer gave his last instructions to the sentries and we started off in the direction of the camp in Gesia Street. I marched at the side of the officer, who had the rank of lieutenant. We marched in twos. I guided them along a way I knew only too well, having crossed it many times during the course of my work as a 'slave.' Immediately after leaving the depot yard, we came across the corpses of two SS men. They were lying near a big pile of bricks. No doubt they had been killed while attempting to make their escape. We took their weapons. Quite a lot of weapons and ammunition were scattered about on that road.

"Slowly we moved forward, examining each pile of stones carefully to see if Germans were hiding behind them. Then we scattered along a front about fifty yards wide, gradually making our way toward Gesia Street. When we were near enough to distinguish the buildings at Pawiak Prison, we heard the noise of footsteps coming in our direction.

"The lieutenant ordered us to hide in the ruins. 'If they are Germans,' he whispered, 'don't fire until you receive the order.'

"We did as he said, the footsteps all the while coming closer and closer. From the noise of the boots ringing out loudly in the silence of the night, it was obvious that they were Germans.

Indeed, soon we saw, less than twenty yards from where we were, six SS men armed with machine guns. It was clear that the partisans besieging the camp had had to fall back for the moment. So the camp and our comrades were still in the hands of the Germans.

"When the enemy patrols were a good way off and we could return to the point from which we had come, the lieutenant immediately had the sentry posts reinforced.

" 'The Germans have considerable forces at their disposal. They could still attack us,' he said.

"The next day my comrades and I all left for Pokorna Street and Bonifraterska Street, where they were beginning to put up barricades and prepare for the battle."

For a long time we are silent. They are probably all thinking of those days not so long ago when all of Warsaw came out into the streets to fight the Germans. How near to victory we thought we were then!

Suddenly Isaac says: "My God, those were unforgettable days. We had a gun in our hands, we felt we had become men again. It was as though we were drunk; we were free, happy. Do you remember the streets of Warsaw? The whole population was outside. Some of them were putting up barricades, others were running to join fighting units, boys of ten or twelve were throwing bottles of gasoline at the German tanks. The women never stopped cooking for the insurgents. . . ."

We see ourselves again on the barricades, weapons in hand. The memory of the past gives us strength. But soon our enthusiasm dies down; our voices grow weaker and then fade out completely. . . .

The sky is white with dawn. Night, our benefactress, she who protects and consoles us, who helps us to live, she is no more. A new day dawns, heavy with menace. Silently each one returns to his corner where, curled up like a bundle of old rags, he will become a still darker blot in that dark bunker, alone with his thoughts.

eleven

Today Hannah cannot sleep. She is concerned about the Jews in the other bunker. She thinks about them all the time. She decides to see for herself what their living conditions are like. She whispers in Samek's ear: "Tonight I am going out with you."

Hannah's presence in the bunker has been an excellent influence on all of us. First, she is kind; and second, her femininity compels us to maintain a certain standard of behavior, thereby giving us self-respect. We control ourselves better in moments of anger and we are generally more careful in our conduct. We force ourselves to maintain a certain level of cleanliness and decency. Hannah has managed to win our esteem and regard because of her sincerity and sensitivity, her charming smile which she can maintain even in the most distressing situations.

At the start of our underground existence her spirit seemed crushed. She would stay for hours on end in her corner, motionless, without saying a word. Often she would weep. We were certain that she would not be able to endure the hard life of the bunker. Then suddenly she pulled herself together and changed so radically that it is she who now scolds us when we become downcast. "There are people worse off than us," she reminds us. "Above all else, we must not let ourselves be discouraged. This is the only way we shall hold out to the very end."

And because we feel ashamed before her, we make an effort to get over our discouragement and our morale improves.

But there are times when Hannah is a stumbling block for us, a source of serious complications. She is twenty, tall, slim, and pretty. She is always neat, her hair well groomed; a charming girl among seven men still reasonably young—to say nothing of Daniel, the youngest among us, our Benjamin. It is true that Samek's presence (he is considered by all as her future husband) helps a great deal to make our relations more normal. There is less strain than if she were alone and free.

All the same, a certain tension occasionally arises as a result of Hannah's presence. After all, we have experienced other things besides life in a bunker with its dreams and nightmares, with its incessant fear of discovery and capture. If we lived the whole time at the mercy of such apprehensions we would perhaps not experience any of life's normal demands; but then we would end by giving way to madness or stupor.

More than once, we actually manage to act, think, and feel like free men. On returning from our expeditions, when we bring something back with us, we frequently eat Hannah's soup with much satisfaction. During these meals, we joke and laugh heartily. At such moments, we become normal once more, we recover our former habits, our natural physical needs. Evidently our looks and actions sometimes betray our thoughts and feelings, for Hannah notices them. Quickly she tries to find something to do to divert our interest from her. Samek too tries to be discreet in her relations with her, so as not to irritate us or rouse in us a feeling of jealousy.

Another complication: at night when we set off in search of supplies, one of us has to stay with Hannah. We always choose unanimously who is to go and who is to stay. Although we have complete confidence in each other, we avoid creating painful situations or conflicts which might soon exert a harmful influence on the whole group and break our will to survive.

Up to now we have managed to surmount these difficulties.

This particular evening Hannah is the first to get up. When we are ready to go about our respective tasks, she announces: "I'm coming with you."

We look at her in astonishment.

"What's the matter?" she asks, smiling. "Do you think you are the only ones who can go out each night? I want to go for a little walk too."

Samek explains that she wants to see the Jews in the other bunker.

Isaac goes with them, and Haskel undertakes to prepare our meal. When we return some hours later, we find three of the men from the other bunker. Hannah has invited them to have a look at our hiding place. We gaze at them and realize that they are completely worn out.

Hurwitz, one of the three, tells us that during his stay in hiding in one of the "Aryan" districts of the city, he thought of his family with such intensity that he feared it would drive him mad.

"In my solitude I would often envy the fate of my wife and children. At least they have left all the torture we suffer behind them. But what is there left for me to do? I often thought of killing myself, but it was impossible for me to bring myself to do it, if only for the sake of those who had sheltered me—my corpse would have been a great embarrassment to them. Then came the insurrection. I didn't hesitate a second. I joined the first armed group I met in the street."

He thinks for a moment, then continues.

"How good that felt! I felt I had become a man again! All the anger burning inside me was released. Nothing seemed impossible to me during the fighting." Then he sighs deeply. "I had no luck. I survived. Whatever you do, you have to be lucky."

"So many Jews fell during the insurrection," I remark. "Hundreds, thousands perhaps came out then from their hiding places. They left the forests, they were set free from the camps. If they had all thought as you do, we would never get very far."

"In any case, we shall never see the end," he says. Then he turns to Wasserman, one of his companions. "Do you remember the day when the fighting ended and we went down into our bunker? How good our morale was then! We were certain that almost immediately—or at least quite soon—we would see the Red Army, and that we would go and join it to drive out the Germans. But the Red Army did not come. Here we are in November and there's still no sign of it. It is cold, winter is coming, and we dare not budge. You can't live on good morale alone."

"Well, stay with us, then," Hannah tells him in a very decisive tone.

Hurwitz looks at her and smiles. "And what have you got here?" Then he is silent, but we guess what he is thinking.

"I know you are sincere, that you are inviting us out of kindness," Wasserman intervenes, trying to alleviate the painful impression his companion's pessimism may have made on us. "But there are ten of us and"—he looks around the bunker—"there would not be enough room for us all even to sit down. Besides, don't think Hurwitz is always as dejected as he is now. We are still hoping too."

It is late. Our visitors get up to leave. "They

won't take us alive," Hurwitz says. "And they'll pay dearly if they ever discover our whereabouts."

"Tomorrow we'll come and see you!" Ignace shouts to them as he says good-bye.

Since then every night someone from our bunker goes to see Wasserman and his companions. Kazik too has been to see them.

In November nature is very capricious. One day the weather is icy and you think you are already in winter's grip. Then suddenly this grip is relaxed, and once more there is rain and mud. This is exactly the way it is during the November we live in our bunker.

We get up one night and make ourselves ready for a foraging expedition. Hannah hastens to prepare the meal, for we are having guests, some of our comrades from the other bunker. It is not the first time we have had visitors, but for us such moments are always occasions for celebration. Usually they send three, for our bunker is too small to hold any more.

Isaac and Daniel are the first to make their way to the bunker entrance. When Isaac takes away the last brick concealing the entrance he is dazzled by a sparkling whiteness. He cries out in surprise and noisily puts the brick back in its place.

It is snow. The yard is completely covered with snow. We cannot go out; our footprints would betray our presence.

The snow has made prisoners of all who still hide in bunkers. It is their enemy; it prevents them from searching for food. Because of the snow, all who have so far survived in bunkers may die of hunger.

"Hurwitz was right when he said the snow would soon fall and that then we would not be able to live on our morale alone," grumbles Haskel.

"There you are, starting again. Always looking on the black side," Ignace says loudly. "What are you trying to do—rub salt into our wounds?"

"Don't shout like that!" Isaac breaks in.

A feeling of panic has set in among us. Although Kazik is upset too, he tries to calm us.

"In November it could still rain. . . . "

"We must not lose hope," Hannah says. "We have enough provisions to last us for some days yet." And immediately she starts preparing the dinner.

"We ought to cut down on our rations," I suggest.

The atmosphere in the bunker is just like that of our first day here, when the house suddenly collapsed on top of us, cutting off all means of exit to the world. With this difference, however: then the fear of dying of hunger in a bunker gave us the strength to act; with our bare hands we tore away bricks, moved away the remnants of walls; we worked without respite, without feeling fatigue. But today fear of the snow seems to have crushed us completely; we feel that it is not just one house but several which have collapsed on our heads and covered us with suffocating debris. This thin layer of snow plunges us into despair because we are defenseless against it. All we can do is to lie on the ground and be patient. It is this feeling of helplessness which we find so overwhelming.

Hannah and Daniel announce jokingly: "Dinner is served!"

"Have you reduced the rations already?" Isaac asks Hannah, breaking the gloomy silence.

"How did you discover that?" Hannah asks in astonishment. "Everyone has as much soup as usual!"

I try to cheer up my companions by remarking: "Oh, there's just one little potato less. What does that matter?"

"Of course, one potato less is nothing. But when it's one out of two. . . ."

"Well, it was Chaim who suggested cutting the rations," Hannah says.

"You don't need to apologize," Samek tells

her. "If the snow goes on falling, we might even be reduced to sharing one potato among all of us. We could even live for a certain time on a plain broth with a little flour added. We still have a few pounds of flour, haven't we?"

"You're forgetting the oats!" Ignace says triumphantly. "When I brought those oats back didn't you say, Isaac, that it was only good for horses? Well, we shall be the horses!"

"We're more to be pitied than horses," Haskel murmurs, clipping his words as usual.

"And were you better off in Pawiak?" I ask angrily. "Remember, you yourself told us how you lay on your bunk while the jailer walked back and forth near your cell. You said that his steps rang out so loudly because of his hobnailed boots that you felt that your head would burst. So you were better off then, eh? You told us how each morning at daybreak you could hear the Gestapo and the SS opening cells and dragging out prisoners. You could hear the poor wretches crying, and the noise of shots in the yard. And every time you heard the footsteps of those Germans in the corridor, you thought your turn had come! Did you think that you would ever get out of there? Eh, Haskel, admit it. A similar stroke of luck could happen to us still! The Red Army could pour into the streets of Warsaw and then we would be free!"

I do not know if my words convince him or

any of the others. But I do know that I have to speak, if only to convince myself that we are still able to survive.

Night is drawing to a close. Daniel climbs to the entrance and once more lifts up the bricks to see if the snow is beginning to melt.

"I think the weather is getting milder," he announces, trying to console us. And he adds smilingly: "If the sun would only put in an appearance, we could certainly go out tomorrow night."

Then he makes his way back down.

We put out the lamp. Each of us lies in his corner. I ask myself: How much longer? Just how long can we hold out? It is time this is over; otherwise the strongest of us risks collapse.

It is only much later, in full daylight, that I finally manage to fall asleep.

twelve

Isaac is on guard. He wakes each of us quietly.

"Something is moving up there."

The noise gets louder. We hear the barking of a dog. This is not the first time we have heard suspicious sounds. Sometimes words shouted in German have reached our ears from the street. At first this used to alarm us considerably. But since it has happened many times now, we have come to the conclusion that this shouting comes from German patrols on their way down to the Vistula.

Now through the grating, which is about level with the ground and looks out onto the street, we hear the rhythmic tread of German boots becoming more and more distinct. We can make out movement near the house above us. The Germans keep coming and going in the yard, as if they are looking for something.

"Last night we were afraid of dying of hunger," Haskel mutters. "Oh no, we won't do that. We won't die of hunger. They've found our hiding place and they'll soon be coming to drag us out."

Ignace too is in despair. He walks about the bunker, talking to himself softly. "It's all over, this is the end. Misfortunes, you are finished forever!"

Our nerves are so much on edge that Ignace's

whispering becomes impossible to bear. Isaac loses his temper and snaps: "What are you carrying on like that for? Do you want them to hear you?"

The priest goes down into the underground passage and starts to pray. Daniel takes up a position near the entrance to try and catch the noises coming from outside; he is anxious to find out whether the Germans are really making their way to our bunker. Samek puts his arm around Hannah to support her; she is trembling. They make for the exit leading to the canal. Isaac and I join Daniel to try and hear what is going on outside. Haskel does not move from his corner; he seems resigned already, indifferent to anything that might happen. "Sooner or later," he mutters. "What does it matter?"

A dull numbness descends upon us. We are all certain that this is the end. The canal on which we were counting as an escape route in case of danger from the outside is now no longer usable because of the cold weather. At the very most we might be able to hold out a few days. Perhaps one single day, just enough to escape some heavy bombardment. But if the bunker is destroyed and we are forced to take refuge in the canal, it will be certain death for us all.

The barking of the dogs nearly drives us mad. We are sure that the Germans have brought these dogs to track us down.

And suddenly, in the midst of that terrible fear, it occurs to me that the Germans might not be concerned with us at all. Perhaps they know nothing of our existence and are engaged in something altogether different. Immediately this supposition seems to me to be an extremely logical one. I remind myself that we did not leave the bunker the night before, so no one could have noticed anything. There had been neither movement nor noise which might have drawn anyone's attention to us.

In a whisper I confide my impression to Isaac, who is the nearest to me. He is trembling uncontrollably.

"Perhaps you are right," he replies.

The Germans prowl nearby for several hours. We remain motionless. Suddenly a violent noise, like an explosion, tears us from our stillness and we all rush toward the canal entrance, so sure are we that they are about to destroy our bunker. Bewildered, we barely manage to find the way. We do not know what direction we are going in; nor are we quite clear from which direction the noise is coming.

Only when the noise is repeated do we grasp what is happening. It is not coming from overhead, from the house above our bunker, but from a wall which looks out onto the street. This wall separates the two parts of a destroyed house. Immediately after the second explosion, the barking of the dogs becomes very loud and then gradually fades away. We hear panic-stricken cries, which in their turn fade away also. We are still at the entrance to the canal, ready to rush into it; but now there is silence again up above. We still do not understand what has happened. We wait a few hours more. Only then do we breath more freely.

"I don't know whose God helped us—that of Kazik or that of Ignace," Hannah says, trying to cheer us up. "They were both praying all the time."

We reply with feeble smiles. We are too exhausted to react in any other way. All of us have only one thought in mind: to lie down and calm our nerves, which are strained to the breaking point; to sleep, if we only can.

Deathly silence reigns now in the bunker. Each of us tries to breathe as quietly as possible. Suddenly in the middle of this silence Kazik, who is lying near the grating, cries out wildly:

"Gas!"

He has a terrible fit of coughing, as though he is choking. He cannot stop coughing, but he puts his hand over his mouth so that his coughing will not be heard from outside. All of us leap up. Yes, we can smell something very strange. The air is rapidly becoming stifling. The smell drifting down from the grating pervades the entire bunker.

"Gas bombs!" Ignace says, as he makes his way down to the canal. We follow him, wanting to get as far away as possible from the entrance, to escape the stifling fumes. This time we are neither wild nor desperate. It seems that we have become indifferent to everything; indeed, we are too exhausted even to be afraid. The poisonous air follows us into the canal, but there it is not as dangerous, for the dampness and the mud absorb it and the huge expanse of the canal diffuses and dilutes it.

So we remain in the sewer, straining our ears to catch the slightest sound, not saying a word.

After a certain time we decide to go back to the bunker. Isaac and I are the first to return. Nothing seems to have changed; but there is still a rather nasty smell in the air.

Isaac climbs toward the entrance which looks out onto the yard and removes the bricks. He takes a good look; there is no trace of any human presence. The snow is unmarked. I stay near the grating a little while. But no suspicious noise reaches my ears. We call our friends.

It is night now. We light the lamp. This time the bunker looks quite different to us; this filthy, stuffy hole looks like home, a place where we can relax and feel welcome.

But we are not completely at ease. What happened outside? What was the meaning of the explosion? Although it is night we cannot go outside to find out. We are held prisoners by the snow.

"It would have been better not to rush into the canal like that," Haskel remarks. "What can we hope for now by staying here?"

"Oh please, Haskel, don't start again," Daniel retorts. "Times like this are hard, but you only make them more difficult if every time there is an alarm you start to give up hope."

"Daniel is right," Hannah adds, a trace of anger in her voice. "It is just another bad moment we've been through."

Ignace looks at her. "Just a bad moment, is that all?" His voice is bitter. "And what next? You might as well say that the rest of our lives is going to be one long bad moment. What is there to hope for? A world in ruins!"

"I am going to make something to eat," Hannah says, and gets up quickly.

Our provisions are running very short. The next day there is the usual artillery duel. We wait impatiently for nightfall, hoping that the snow will melt and we shall be able to go search for food and find out the reasons for the explosions.

But the snow is still there, pure and smooth. Our anxiety is so great that we avoid entering into conversation with one another. The snow has become our greatest enemy.

Three days later, Isaac climbs down from the observation post without saying a word and goes to where our provisions are kept. He examines them and shakes his head. We understand what that means. The situation is desperate.

Two days later, in the afternoon, Ignace notices water falling drop by drop. Drops of water penetrate our shelter through the cracks between the bricks. Ignace goes wild with joy. He puts his head under the drops to convince himself that the snow is melting at last. When he is quite convinced of this, he makes his way down to us, wakes us up one by one, and tells us. The few hours that separate us from nightfall seem endless.

As soon as it is dark, Isaac and I make our way out into the open and head for the place where we heard the explosion a few days before. There we see broken glass strewn on the ground along the road leading to the cellar of a neighboring house. Inside the cellar we see the traces of an explosion. It appears that the Germans found containers full of some chemical. While moving the containers, the soldiers must have broken two of them. The spilled liquid had flowed toward our grating. This was the explanation of the disagreeable smell which had made us rush out of our bunker, and which we had taken to be gas. The Germans had not exploded gas bombs; they had not discovered our bunker. We hurry back to inform our comrades.

We have all found new strength. Everyone wants to take part in the foraging expedition. Kazik, our priest, affirms vigorously: "I'm going too. I am feeling extremely well and I don't want exceptions to be made in my case."

"Don't let's waste more time," Isaac says. "The snow will be here again soon and perhaps it will go on all winter. We have to bring back everything we can lay our hands on. We can't be choosy. We can't even turn our nose up at rotten potatoes!"

It is my turn to remain behind with Hannah. They are nearly all outside when Hannah shouts: "Will one of you go and see the Jews in the other bunker?"

"We'll go without fail if there is any chance at all of doing so," Samek says reassuringly.

It is very late when they return. They apologize and say they were forced to cover quite a distance. Everyone of them has brought back many things. During the meal there is much good humor. We laugh and joke and tease each other gently. But Hannah is a little bit sulky; she is rather cross with Samek. He did not keep his promise to go to the other bunker. He tried to but heard suspicious noises which could have come from German patrols; he was forced to turn back.

At daybreak we lie down as usual. About ten o'clock in the morning, Kazik wakes us cautiously. "I can hear footsteps in the canal."

When Isaac and I climb toward the entrance, the footsteps are already very close to our bunker. Soon we hear a voice say in Polish: "Don't be afraid. It's me, Joseph Bednarski."

A second later we can see him crawling toward us. Joseph Bednarski is one of the three Resistance fighters that we had met in the canal going to Zoliborz while the fighting was still going on there. It is difficult to imagine our joy when we recognize him—a representative from the world of the living!

Joseph tells us he has come to see if we are still alive. If he had been less pessimistic about us, he might have brought us some food. He tells us that the Germans have taken all the insurgents to Prushkow and from there have sent them to various camps in Germany. He himself has managed to join a platoon that the Germans send to Warsaw each day to search the ruins for objects which might be useful to them. And because he speaks German, he has become a sort of vice-captain of his troop.

"You never told us you spoke German," Isaac remarks.

"I never had the chance to tell you before," Joseph says, as though justifying himself. "But there is no need to be afraid." Then, turning to

Isaac and putting his hand on his shoulder, he insists:

"You can trust me! No one has seen me, no one knows where I am. We are working a long way from here. My Germans think I have gone looking to see where any useful objects can still be found. They let me move about freely."

"Exactly where did you come down into the canal?" I ask him.

"Not far from here there's a hole in the wall. It was made during the uprising because we needed it. This hole leads to one of the lateral canals. I came down through there, then I made my way toward the principal canal in order to get here. I'll come back tomorrow and bring you something to eat."

It is already late and Joseph leaves us. At noon the guards come back and he must be there on time. Isaac goes part way with him. He wants to see if what Joseph has said about the lateral canal is true.

When Joseph has gone, we feel rather strange. We are pleased that someone still remembers us, but we cannot help feeling a certain mistrust of Joseph. Isn't it just possible he might have come to spy on us? The fact that he can leave his platoon in that way and make off on his own arouses our suspicions. But after a day has passed our mistrust of Bednarski diminishes somewhat.

That night there are noises that indicate activity in the neighborhood of our bunker. We hear the shouting which usually accompanies the movements of German patrols. When this happens, we abandon our expeditions and stay all night in the bunker.

We take advantage of this night's rest to take stock of the provisions we brought back the previous night; we sieve them to remove the sand and the straw. We found some dried peas, various other dried vegetables, pearl barley, oats, and a handful or two of rice. We now pick out the rice grain by grain to separate it from the sand. This takes us all night. When we discover a few dried beans among our "trophies," there is general jubilation. As for Bednarski, we are now convinced he means us no harm.

Hannah talks constantly about the Jews in the other bunker. The next night Isaac and I make our way toward Kozla Street. Crouched behind the rubble of a house, we strain our ears to make sure all is quiet so we can cross the road.

"Do you think Hannah is wrong to worry about them?" Isaac whispers. "Something really must have happened to them. Why did they never come to see us again?"

"We shall soon know," I say, getting ready to cross the road.

Isaac pulls me back by the sleeve. "Wait. If

they have been taken, it is quite possible a German patrol has been stationed nearby to surprise possible callers."

We stay there for some time in the shelter of the ruins. All sorts of theories about the possible fate of our friends occur to us. But there is no question of going back until we are certain exactly what has happened to them. Quickly, we cross the road. Once we reach the yard, we stop and listen intently for a long time. When we are certain there is no one around, we slip inside the yard. We stop once more, looking cautiously before we advance, step by step, to where their bunker is situated. We are just about to utter the word "Shalom," when we see it is no longer necessary. The pile of stones, bricks, and gravel which had been put there to conceal the entrance to the bunker has been pushed aside. And in the bunker itself—there is no one!

We can stay no longer. Without exchanging a word, we hurry back up to our bunker. When Hannah and Samek see we have returned so early—empty-handed—they quickly guess the truth. Tears run down Hannah's face. When Ignace returns and hears the news, he cries like a child.

thirteen

Five days have passed since Joseph Bednarski's visit. We are all convinced that he will not come again. Each of us finds a different reason to explain his visit. Someone offers a strange hypothesis: "Perhaps Bednarski thought we were all dead already, so he came down here to get hold of our belongings."

One thing is certain: he did not come to betray us to the Germans. We are soon to find out that in fact Joseph Bednarski tries each day to make his way down to us with some food. But he cannot manage it. He cannot leave when he wants to because he is afraid of being followed. But at last his opportunity comes.

Inside the bunker we hear someone in the canal whistling a tune and shouting some reassuring words. Ignace, who is on guard, immediately signals that Bednarski is coming.

It is about ten o'clock in the morning. He comes into the bunker and pulls out from under his belt two round loaves of bread. Then he turns out his pockets and out fall some onions and a packet of lard. At the sight of bread, which we have not eaten for so many months, out eyes open wide in wonder.

Joseph is afraid to stay too long. We tell him of the disappearance of the Jews from the other bunker. He tells us that the platoons of forced laborers are sent much less often into the ruins now; they come only for a few hours in the morning. The Germans are reinforcing their positions near the Vistula, but they do not wish this to be too obvious. Joseph advises us to be very careful when we go out foraging at night; the Germans are constantly on the move and each time they establish new strongpoints. It is particularly convenient for them to do so here in the ruins where there are no people.

Before he goes, he promises to come again if he can. Then he disappears rapidly into the canal.

That evening, when Hannah holds out a plate of soup to Daniel, he says to her, smiling: "I didn't expect such a royal menu!"

This soup cannot be compared to the kind we have every day. Hannah has minced an onion and has fried it a golden brown with a little of the lard. So our soup has quite a different color and a different taste. And what a delicious aroma! In addition, Hannah gives each of us a piece of bread. Truly, this is a menu for a king.

Kazik is radiant—his pleasure can be seen on his face—because it is a Pole who has helped us. What Joseph has done is, in his eyes, some measure of redemption for all the harm so many Poles did to the Jews. He communicates this to us by a gentle allusion which he slips in between two spoonfuls of soup: "Among all nations, in every generation, there are noble, courageous men."

We too are very satisfied. This action by a Pole seems to us a foretaste of things to come.

And Joseph comes to see us again. This time, besides food he brings a Polish newspaper. During the night Isaac reads it to us. We hear the names of towns and villages, and we have the feeling of being linked once more with the world of the living, which we have almost forgotten.

Joseph's visits are of inestimable value to us. He comes two or three times a week and he never comes empty-handed. Each time he brings us something to eat, as well as various newspapers—and accounts of things that cannot even be found in the newspapers. We, in our turn, try to do all we possibly can for him. We know he is without funds, so we give him various objects we have found on our nightly excursions. He hides them under his clothes and, once outside, manages to sell them.

He comes again in December and tells us to be extremely careful, because the Germans are making great preparations; so much so that he wonders if they are expecting powerful reinforcements. It is possible that soldiers might be posted here in our very yard. Even now, platoons of forced laborers come rarely into the ruins; soon they will no doubt stop coming altogether. Then he leaves.

During the days that follow this last visit, we still hope to see him again; he will come tomorrow, the day after, perhaps. But after a week we lose all hope.

(After our liberation we went straight to his house in Prushkow. His wife told us that he had been hit when a shell exploded while he was in Warsaw with his platoon, and that he did not recover from his wounds.)

In December the risk of being caught by the Germans increases daily. They are concentrating their troops in Warsaw to reinforce their positions. German detachments move constantly about the ruins. In spite of this, we go out every night to try to build up reserves of food. We are convinced that we shall have to spend the winter in our bunker and we fear the snow. For the moment, it is content to put in brief appearances, but there will be a day when it will come to stay for good, and then we shall be endlessly confined. So we take everything we can lay our hands on back to our refuge, and we reduce our rations more and more, so as to be able to hold out as long as possible.

Haskel, our steward, announces that we have enough provisions to be able to hold out for several more weeks. We have by now become so adept at avoiding enemy soldiers that we are almost insensitive to the threat of being left with no food. One night we are making the usual preparations for our foraging expedition. We begin to remove the bricks which conceal the entrance in order to slip outside where all seems calm. Suddenly we hear the footsteps of a detachment of soldiers heading toward our yard. Then we hear the clatter of objects flung to the ground and the jumble of conversations in German. Quickly we replace the bricks, put out the light, and without making any kind of meal whatsoever we lie silent for the rest of the night.

They leave our yard the next day. And then, as if nothing had happened, we set off at once to look for food among the ruins and in the cellars. The struggle for survival and our familiarity with danger blind us to the mortal peril we risk every time we go out.

Quite often, in the darkness of the night, I lean my head outside the bunker. Sometimes I even sit up on the bricks and gaze at the darkness, which is pierced by powerful searchlights on the other side of the Vistula. By their light, I am able to glimpse the ruins. Every time a luminous beam sweeps through space, I instinctively put my head down and hunch my shoulders, so as not to be dazzled by the point of light and also so as not to be seen. I am beginning to think that among the ruins of Warsaw everything is the reverse of things in normal life; it is light which can bring evil spirits down on us, in the shape of the Nazis, and it is the darkness which protects us from them. I have even become indifferent to the constant running and screeching of the rats.

From time to time my companions too make their way up to the entrance to remain for a moment in the darkness, alone with themselves.

Inside the bunker, none of us is alone. We never do anything without talking about it to the others. And yet our being forced to live this communal life brings a desire for solitude; we need to be alone, even for just a few minutes, to think on our own, not to have anyone about. And here, on the bricks near the exit, is the ideal place for a nocturnal moment of solitude; here, each of us can let his thoughts wander as far away as he pleases. . . .

Isaac and Daniel have so thoroughly perfected the art of scouring the cellars that they never come back empty-handed. In the course of one of their searches, they once even come quite close to the advance German army units along the Vistula. They manage to elude them, though not without difficulty.

One night they are busy clearing a mound of debris to see if it conceals some useful object when they notice a huge glass flask wrapped in straw. Paraffin containers are usually wrapped like this in Poland. Besides, this flask is covered with rags, which are always most useful to us.

At first Daniel does not want to examine the

flask too closely. "What's the good of taking paraffin back to the bunker?"

But Isaac gets it into his head that he wants to smell it; so he pulls off the cork. . . .

It is brandy!

They return immediately to the bunker, breathless, elated, as though they had found a treasure. It really is an excellent contribution. It is extremely cold, we really have very little to eat, and the brandy warms and strengthens us.

This brandy becomes particularly precious to us when, about December 10, the frost puts in an appearance and snow settles over the city.

The snow shuts us in as though we were in a cage. We are already very weak after three months of life in the bunker. Not only do we suffer from physical exhaustion, but our nerves are at the breaking point. The nights are particularly hard to bear. Often we get up, look at each other, and do not know what to do or say. At certain moments our boredom becomes so unbearable that it rises in our throats and clutches at our hearts. Our high morale—which was our greatest asset—begins to decline. I think of all this as I watch Isaac nervously take a turn around the bunker. Ignace sits in his corner, his head in his hands. As for Samek, his eyes are fixed on the ceiling. If this state of affairs lasts much longer we shall be in great danger of losing our senses.

At moments like this a single word can put our nerves on edge, provoke quarrels, make us fight among ourselves. Soon we shall be reduced to fasting. I am afraid that even among the best of us, hunger may arouse our basest instincts. Perhaps the last of our food reserves will provoke quarrels.

Fortunately for us, the deep understanding forged between us through the months of communal existence resists all assaults upon it. Not once do we argue over food, however much hunger gnaws at our insides.

But there are moments when we do quarrel and raise our voices at each other. This usually occurs in the course of the discussions we have during the nights we cannot go out. For each of us has very decided opinions; each of us passes judgment on and analyzes events according to his own views. Some of us show a total lack of interest in the postwar world, from which we expect nothing good. Those who think like this believe men have grown accustomed to evil and will remain that way. Others think that a lesson will be learned from all the evil and that past events will teach men to be decent.

We try to avoid discussions like these, so as not to create an atmosphere of discord. We endeavor to preserve our understanding and good feeling. We know that our survival depends upon it. And yet our fears are far from disappearing. We all know full well that if the present state of affairs continues, even if no one discovers our hiding place and no shell or bomb lands on us, we still cannot hold out for long.

We have very little food. The thought of starving to death terrifies us. Such a death seems to us the most atrocious of all. Our anguish at the thought of it is so deep-rooted that it becomes a continual torment to us. Sleep—our only relaxation—escapes us. As soon as night falls, Haskel lights the stove and puts the end of the pipe outside to let out the smoke. Then one of us climbs up to the entrance to waft the smoke away, to disperse it, so it cannot be seen from a long way off. The others remain seated in the half-darkness, and watch the fire. As we have to economize on acetylene, we only light the lamp in cases of absolute necessity.

So we spend hours and hours staring in silence at the fire, each of us plunged into his own thoughts.

After some weeks of total seclusion because of the snow, I realize that we are in the grip of utter despair and hopelessness. The prospect of an early liberation and the hope of being saved recede farther and farther into the distance. Conversations about this prospect and hope slowly become less frequent, and then die out completely.

After a night spent around the stove deep in

terrible thoughts, Isaac and Daniel will leap up suddenly and drink a good mouthful of brandy from the flask. Apparently they want to stupefy themselves, to stop themselves from thinking and forget their troubles. Sometimes they overdo it—so much so that they forget where they are and start singing at the tops of their voices. When we lecture them for risking bringing trouble down on us all, they subside and burst out sobbing.

All of us are increasingly terrified at the thought of a slow, protracted death. I am no longer indifferent to the cries of the rats. Although we are used to them, I quiver with fear each time I hear them. I can already picture myself on the ground with no strength left to move, while the rats swarm over me. Various ideas torment me, plans for escaping outside drift across my mind, plans which I reject one after another. How can I get out of here, and where can I go?

Once, as we are all sitting around the fire, I express my thoughts aloud. I tell them that if the situation continues for much longer, and if our supplies of food run out, I do not intend to stay there and wait for death. I shall leave.

"I'll go with you," Daniel says, without hesitation.

"And where will you go?" Ignace asks. "You want to go looking for death, Chaim?"

"It's better than sitting here waiting for it," Isaac sighs.

"Why shouldn't we all try to get out of here?" I argue. "We could make our way through the cellars and try to get out of the city."

I try to convince them; or is it myself I am trying to convince?

"And if you did succeed in getting out of the city, who would give you shelter?" Haskel grumbles.

"Today everybody would be willing to take us in," I say, still trying to defend my idea.

"You are living in a dream world. Do you think everything has changed already?" Hannah intervenes.

"What is your opinion, Kazik?" I ask our priest.

Kazik starts to stammer; his reply is not clear. I understand him. After staying among us so long, he refuses to admit the truth. No one would help us even if we succeed in leaving Warsaw. My companions reject my idea.

"It can't work. The town is on the front line."

"We can't reach the other end of Warsaw through the cellars."

"We would have to take to the streets, and we would certainly be caught."

However, all of us are consumed with the idea, convinced we have to find a way of getting out of here. And it has its effect. Our reflections take another turn, a turn for the better. Now we are trying to solve the problem of how to survive, rather than passively waiting for death.

We work out a plan to escape across the Vistula and join the Soviet Army at Praga. We first thought about this when we heard the sound of mouth organs from the other side of the river about a month after we came to live in the bunker. But then there was no way of getting across the river. Now our plan seems more feasible. It is extremely cold, and if the temperature drops still more, as usually happens in Poland in January, the Vistula will soon freeze. We could reach the Vistula through the main sewer and cross the front by sliding on our stomachs.

We cannot complete all the details of our plan, for it is nearly day. We must end our conversation and lie down. But from now on we have something to keep us going, a new preoccupation, an idea to which we can cling.

The following night, Isaac puts before us a finished plan. He talks about it with great assurance, as though there is not a shadow of a doubt that it can be carried out successfully.

"Everybody knows," he states, "that the sewers empty into the Vistula. So it is certain that the main canal will lead us there."

"And what if the Germans are there? It is right there that they have reinforced their positions and dug trenches. How shall we get out of the canal? They'll spot us right away!" Ignace argues.

"Oh, come now," Isaac replies. "No one digs trenches near water. They are dug quite a distance away. They won't see us."

"What about the searchlights?" Hannah asks him. The Soviet Army continually focuses lights on this side of the Vistula so they can see what preparations the Germans are making for an attack; and the Germans illuminate the other bank of the river to see what is going on there. "What about them?" Hannah asks again.

Isaac thinks for a moment, then responds. "We'll have to be dressed in white. We'll have to lengthen our clothes so they cover us completely. We can also use the sheet that covers the entrance to our shelter to wrap around us. When the searchlights are on, we'll remain completely still, flattened against the snow, so we won't be seen. As soon as it's dark again, we'll crawl forward. Then, when we reach the other side, I'll shout out in Russian that we are Jews, and they won't fire on us. You'll see, it will work," Isaac concludes with assurance.

Everyone is satisfied with this plan—except Haskel, who mutters: "We'll be frozen before we get across."

No one answers him.

Now Isaac turns to me. "Chaim, come down

with me into the canal. We have to explore a bit and see what route to take."

"I'll come with you," Daniel says.

"When you get back, dinner will be ready," Hannah says. "At least what we've got left."

"Don't be too stingy with the water," Daniel says, grinning.

The way to the Vistula through the canal is very long, and we do not know exactly where the canal empties into the river. Is it near the broken-down bridge that joins the Cracovian Suburb to Praga; is it near the other bridges, which are also in ruins; or is it simply on the edge of some field? But this is not so important. What is crucial is whether it empties above or below the surface of the river.

We crawl along the canal. Isaac holds a lighted candle which he covers with his hand so that we can see the way by the light of the flame that glows between his fingers.

The nearer we get to the Vistula, the more the danger increases, for above us every inch of the surface is occupied by soldiers. The entire bank is solidly fortified. For hours we are forced to go forward without saying a word. Suddenly we have to stop.

In front of us the canal is blocked by iron bars.

These bars are very long and are placed so as to let the water pass, but they are not wide enough to allow a man to get through. Isaac brings the candle up near the bars. We are able to make out that at this point the canal begins to slope down much more steeply. We realize that it cannot be far to the river. Near the bars we see an iron ladder which leads up to one of the sewer lids. Daniel climbs the ladder and tries to lift the lid, to see what is going on outside. The lid is too heavy; he is able to lift it only a crack. Through the crack comes the sound of heavy boots. He goes back down the ladder and we hurry away from there.

"The bars prove that the Vistula is very close," Isaac explains. "They have been put there to block the passage of the bulky refuse which the canal carries along. Only the water can get through. Later, the sewage workers come along and remove the rest of the waste."

The moment we get back into the bunker, our comrades realize that we have encountered an obstacle to our plan.

"And I thought you were already at Praga!" says Hannah, smiling and trying to cheer us up.

"What? Without you?" Daniel retorts. Then he adds: "Who knows if we shall ever get there."

Isaac says nothing. He sits down, deep in thought. I talk to our friends about the obstacle which stopped us, this grating made of iron bars that cuts off our route to Praga.

It is getting late. Hannah serves our pitiful meal.

"Eat what there is. Soon it will be daylight and we'll be forced to lie down," she urges us.

"Perhaps it's all for the best," Haskel mutters as he stretches out on the ground. "If we do leave the bunker, we risk freezing to death on the ice. Better to die peacefully here."

Nobody answers him. Hannah puts out the light and lies down near Samek.

I am awake a long time. I feel as though I have lost something that might have saved my life. I am depressed and weak. I feel a terrible longing for my home, for my wife and children. Everything looks black to me. All is lost, I tell myself. My heads begins to spin. Nightmarish pictures of all the accumulated horrors I have suffered in the concentration camps refuse to leave me. I find myself shouting and screaming.

"Chaim, what is happening to you?"

I open my eyes and see my friends crowding around me. I bury my head in my rags and feel thoroughly ashamed of myself.

Watching Haskel sharpening his knife on a stone in order to chop the firewood more easily, we have an idea.

"Do you think it would be possible to saw through an iron bar with that knife?" Isaac asks.

"Anything is possible," Haskel replies.

"In that case, come with us," I say to him.

We make our way down again into the canal. Haskel examines the bars with great care. Then he notices the sewer lid above our heads. It is only when we have left the bars a long way behind that he gives us his opinion.

"We can saw through those bars, yes, although they are very thick. It will take time, but we can do it. We have a bit of grease, so we can keep on greasing the blade. Only it makes a loud noise when you saw, and it echoes, especially in a sewer. What will happen if the sentry up above hears us, eh?"

"We can take precautions," Isaac replies. "Tomorrow night we'll come back here. Two of us will go up and lift the cover to see just where the sentry is, whether he moves away, and if so, exactly how far. Then we'll know precisely at what moment we can saw without being heard from the outside."

The following night Haskel is busy cutting out teeth in his knife so it can be used as a saw. He wants to be ready to start work immediately in case circumstances turn out to be favorable.

"It will take a long time to finish this job successfully. We could be dead before it's finished," Haskel tells us.

"You always look on the black side," Hannah says.

"It's also possible that we may be liberated before it's finished," I tell him.

This time four of us go down into the canal. When we reach the grille, Isaac and Daniel climb the iron ladder to the sewer cover and listen intently, trying to make out if the sentry is nearby. In the empty silence of the night, the slightest noise can be heard. There is no one about, and the noise of the studded soles of the sentry's boots reaches us very clearly through the slight gaps in the sewer lid. After succeeding in lifting the lid very slightly, Isaac and Daniel endeavor to find out exactly how far the sentry marches—it is cold and he certainly cannot stay still for very long—and exactly how long he takes to march there and back.

They see the sentry turn to come toward them; they lower the lid and wait. After awhile they ascertain that between the sentry's going and coming, five minutes elapse. So it will be possible to saw for three minutes without running any risk of discovery.

Haskel is waiting below, tool in hand, ready to start sawing the bar. His eyes are fixed on Isaac. The moment Isaac raises his hand, Haskel begins to work. As soon as Isaac repeats the movement, Haskel stops.

During the night, Haskel announces: "Yes, it's coming along very nicely." He has managed to cut through several centimeters of the bar.

At the table that night our joy knows no bounds. Not for a moment do we worry that here in the depth of our bunker we are still in danger and that the success of our plan is far from certain. We joke about the German oaf about us, up there on guard, while down below we are in the middle of sawing an iron bar and bringing to fruition our plan of escape right under his very nose.

It is not the certainty of success which gives us such courage and strength; it is the plan itself and the work it involves. These give us a renewed desire to live. We have shaken off our resignation, our passive waiting for whatever it is fate has in store for us.

We are all working to bring our plan into being. We prepare white clothes to camouflage ourselves in. And we make ropes. Because the canal on the other side of the grille descends very steeply and we are afraid that the slope may become even steeper as it gets near the Vistula, which would make walking very difficult, we decide to make ropes with which we will be able to hold each other up. Not having any real ropes, we make some by plaiting strips of rag which we tie securely end to end.

All these preparations help us to forget the threat of famine which daily reduces our chances of surviving.

The days pass more quickly than before. At

least it seems that they do. Each millimeter of iron bar we successfully cut through is for us a victory, a promise, a joy.

But we cannot saw continually. Before we can start to work, we have to carefully watch the sentry and note the course he takes. We notice that each sentry performs his guard duty in his own way. Some of them keep well away from the sewer cover; others hover around it. In the latter case it is impossible for us to continue sawing—we come all the way for nothing.

One night the sentry moves away and we start to cut through the bar. When we figure that the sentry is back, we stop. Suddenly Daniel and Isaac, who are near the sewer cover, hear him walk quickly and then almost break into a run. They signal to us. We put out the candle. Soon we hear footsteps on the sewer cover itself. The sentry stamps on the cover with his feet. We are convinced that he heard us. What can we do? Should we run? But our footsteps would be heard. So we keep absolutely still. The sentry goes on stamping his feet. Slowly we realize that he is cold and is simply trying to warm himself. We take advantage of the noise he is making to go quietly back to our bunker.

This work and the other preparations that have to be made for our escape to the opposite bank of the Vistula keep us so busy that often in imagination we already see ourselves far away from the bunker. The obstacle in our way has almost been overcome; one of the bars is very near to being completely cut through. All the material we will need to make our way across the frozen Vistula is also ready. Each of us has a pile of rags to wrap around his knees to protect them from the ice. The white clothes, made with sheets that we found in the cellars, are ready. When Isaac tries on his camouflage, wraps himself up in white, even covers up his head, Haskel murmurs: "Well done! We've already got our shrouds. At least we shall die like good Jews!"

Two weeks later, when the blade finally cuts through the bar, a beaming smile lights up Haskel's face and he announces: "The road is clear!"

Had it not been for the sentry up above, we would have shouted for joy. With all our strength we push the bar to one side so as to make the space wider. Isaac tries getting through to the other side and manages it with no difficulty at all. The way is really open.

We return to the bunker. It is late. We swallow the thin soup Hannah has made for us and lie down. It is beginning to get light.

The following night we try to reach the Vistula. To cross the river is impossible for it is not yet frozen. We want only to search out the place where the canal empties into the Vistula to make sure the Germans are not keeping a watch on that particular spot.

We set off in a group of three—Daniel, Isaac, and I. We take a rope in order to hold on to each other in case the slope becomes too steep. We slip between the bars. The way along the canal dips more and more steeply. By holding on to the wall we can still go forward, but only very slowly. The farther we go the deeper the water becomes and the steeper the slope gets. Soon it will be impossible for us to go any farther.

We stop and shine a light onto the canal water in the hope of being able to see the bank of the Vistula. According to our calculations we ought to be very close to it, but we can see no sign of an opening. The light reveals only water; as far as we can see there is water, water—nothing but water. . . .

Daniel says: "I am going on alone."

"What?" I say. "Suppose you cannot get back? The current will pull you away."

"What about the rope? What's that for?" Isaac replies.

"All right," Daniel agrees. "I'll hold the rope by one end and if it gets really impossible to go any farther, I'll shout and you can pull me back."

"No, it's not all right," I insist. "What if he gets too tired? He might let go of the rope."

To tell the truth, I do not want Daniel to try

this. I have become so attached to him that I love him like my own child and I would rather go down into the water myself.

But Daniel insists. "I'll wind the rope around my waist and knot it tightly."

Carefully we tie a rope around Daniel's waist, and he sets off. He walks slowly, leaning against the wall.

Soon we hear him shout: "Quick! Pull me up!"

We begin pulling on the rope. It is with great difficulty that we manage to get him back.

He tells us: "The water is very deep there; it is impossible to stay on your feet. I slipped on the slope. . . ."

He is soaked to the skin and quite exhausted. We almost have to carry him back to the bunker. Isaac and I are worn out too; we drag ourselves along with difficulty.

The hope we had of early freedom has now vanished. All the efforts we have made, all the risks we have taken, all the work we have done—it has all been for nothing. . . .

fourteen

Hannah gets up before everyone else and begins checking our provisions. The night before, while Isaac was in the canal, Hannah reminded us that today is his birthday. We decided to surprise him with a party. That is why Hannah has awakened so early.

Isaac is the most effective and efficient of us all. He is energetic and full of vitality. He explores the cellars for nights on end, risking his life to bring back to the bunker the things necessary to keep us alive. Yet he will never accept anything more than an equal share for himself.

The failure of our plan to escape through the canal, a plan to which Isaac had devoted himself with so much dedication, has had more of an adverse effect upon him than upon the rest of us. The two weeks when we were busy getting ready for our escape passed very quickly. We were so happy each night when we returned from the canal and heard Haskel tell us how much of the bar still remained to be cut through. And those who had remained in the bunker would show us how many yards of rope they had plaited and the clothing they had prepared. So the disappointment is cruel and its effect upon us depressing.

Our provisions are running out. It is impossible to go out at night now, as the snow has set in for good and will not melt until the spring.

Even if we ate the smallest amount possible to keep us alive, it would still mean that there would be a long stretch in which we would have nothing at all left in the way of food. We are now reducing our rations each day in the hope of making our provisions last a little longer. But even this extreme economy cannot put off the end for long. Soon we shall have nothing left to eat.

Isaac feels this more than any of us. He was so convinced that we would succeed in escaping through the sewers. Even now that this plan is abandoned, he often goes down into the canal to the place where the slope becomes very steep to see if the waters have subsided and if there is a possibility of getting through them. Usually he stays there quite a long time, then comes back to the bunker, stretches out on the ground, his eyes fixed on the ceiling, and does not speak to anyone.

Today it is the same thing all over again. Except for Hannah, no one is in a hurry to get up, although it is already night. It is impossible to go out. The snow keeps us prisoners; we are shut in by its whiteness, which we dare not disturb. All the same, Hannah, who has prepared for her cooking a little flour with the usual addition of sand, reminds us that it is time to light the stove. Haskel gets up. Making the fire is his job. I get up too and climb to the entrance to disperse the smoke. I lean outside and feel how bitingly cold it is; only the heat coming from the pipe warms my face. Once more I gaze at the ruins of Warsaw: skeletons which the sparkling snow has clothed in white, impassive witnesses of immense destruction. Mechanically, with the help of a rag, I continue dispersing the smoke while I look toward Praga where people are sleeping —in their beds—the sleep of the free.

When I get back into the bunker, I find it completely transformed. Hannah has covered the table with a white rag, and this gives our shelter an air of festivity. In addition to our thin watery soup—which has been our only dish for quite a while now—Hannah has prepared, with what remains of the sandy flour, a large oven cake, which we devour with our eyes.

Isaac says jokingly: "It is obvious that Hannah wants to marry Samek now, today, before they both die! Who will perform the ceremony? But haven't we a priest among us?"

Hannah smiles and goes on with her preparations.

The fire on our stove begins to burn low. We call Samek, who is on duty up above, dispersing the smoke. The table is set. Hannah brings the remains of the brandy and pours out a little for each of us. Then she puts the flat cake in front of Isaac.

"It's your birthday, Isaac," she says to him.

"Today we are celebrating your birthday in the hope that there will be many more birthdays for you to celebrate."

She kisses him. We all wish him good luck with a resounding: "L'chaim!" We empty our glasses and proceed to do justice to the cake. The sand grates against our teeth.

Isaac is so surprised he cannot say a word. All of a sudden he starts to sob. When he is at last able to control himself he tells us that if we survive, this day will remain the dearest memory for him, something he will never forget.

We talk until dawn. Isaac seems to have taken on new life. All the pain which has weighed upon him in the course of these last few days has disappeared. His face shines, he is a new man. He has managed to regain his self-control. So have we.

Toward the end of December, the daily barrages of gunfire begin to change in nature. They become intermittent. Often whole days pass without a single shot's being fired. But at the beginning of January they start up again. There are incessant artillery duels and frequent attacks from the air. We never know where the bombs will fall. As soon as we hear the throbbing of aircraft, we run for shelter in the canal. This happens several times a day, and it tires us considerably. During the day we can no longer sleep, for often we are forced to remain several hours in the canal.

We cannot understand why the battles have broken out again with such increased violence. But we understand only too well that our days are numbered. The shelling and aerial bombardments have exhausted us. The increasing concentration of German troops in the districts all around us adds to the danger of our being caught and forces us to keep very still night and day. It also prevents us from making a fire. Only occasionally, when we are certain that all is quiet and that there is no one in our yard, does Hannah's face regain its serene expression. Then the stove is lighted, and she prepares something for us to eat.

With each day that passes the soup becomes thinner. Then, on about the 12th or 13th of January, Hannah pours out our soup as usual, with the same cup, into the same plates, but her hand trembles, her face is clouded. She hangs her head as if she does not want to look at anyone.

The soup is only water. Our provisions are exhausted.

At first no one says anything. Each of us begins to swallow his soup.

I glance at Daniel, who is sitting beside me. The last few days he has been feeling weak and he has a slight temperature. I look at Hannah. She is making a great effort to hold back her tears. All the others are sitting there, heads down. This is the end of eight human beings. We are going to die slowly of hunger. Suddenly I feel an enormous pity for all these good people who have managed to maintain a decency and humanity toward each other under such difficult conditions. I hang my head like the others and sink deep into my thoughts—chaotic thoughts. I can see absolutely no way out of our situation.

Ignace heaves a deep sigh and says, as if he were talking to himself: "It really only needs these few victims now, does it, to complete the sacrificial slaughter?"

Perhaps he is addressing this question to God, as he has a habit of doing in moments of distress.

"We will not be the last victims," I reply. "Many others will die before we triumph over the swine responsible for all this destruction."

Daniel groans. "How does it help me if other people perish too? I haven't even lived yet. . . ."

Tears pour down his face. Hannah turns away her head. I stroke Daniel's hair. I would so much like to comfort him but I do not know what to say. After four months of living underground we have no doubt that we shall not survive for long now that we have nothing left to eat.

Isaac, stretched out on the ground, keeps repeating: "If the world at least could know about us. But even if anyone finds the bunker, they will find no trace of us. The rats will have cleaned up everything."

"And what if the world does learn of it?" Samek says. "Would you feel better? At least your sufferings will be over once the rats begin to eat you." Samek is young too, and his words express a deep and bitter suffering.

As usual, Haskel is silent. Perhaps he is reacting to the situation better than the others. For a long time now he has been convinced that we will never get out of here alive. Kazik, our priest, says nothing either. He goes back to his place, kneels down, and murmurs his evening prayers. This time he lingers over them. Perhaps he is begging God to work a miracle for us. Then he covers himself up completely with his coat. But he does not sleep.

Ignace climbs up toward the entrance; it is his turn to be on guard. I cover Daniel with a pile of rags; he is shivering because of the cold. Hannah and Samek are sitting in the darkness very close to each other, talking softly. During these last days they have much to say to each other.

The next day when the firing starts again, we no longer take refuge in the canal. Sooner or later death will overtake us anyway, as Haskel says, so why rush into the sewer? Each time a bomb explodes nearby we sit up; then we lie down again. The atmosphere that prevails in the bunker during these moments defies all description. Is it fear? No, I am no longer afraid. I remember that during the preceding weeks, when danger was imminent from either the canal or the yard, I felt my heart contract and my whole body shudder. Now nothing like this happens to me. My companions show no agitation either. Are we resigned, overwhelmed? Now we know exactly what awaits us. An atmosphere of expectancy reigns in the bunker. We are waiting either for a miracle or for death. There is no other alternative.

Nights are particularly hard to bear. Once the firing ceases we remember our former habits—now we would be eating our meal; now we would be sipping brandy. . . . Hannah approaches the place where we kept our provisions. Perhaps she was mistaken when she said there was nothing left. But, crestfallen, she turns and starts making the fire.

"With a little hot water we can still manage to survive for a time," she says.

"And afterwards?" Ignace asks. "Do you remember when we began to dig our bunker? I said that we were digging a tomb to bury ourselves in alive. No one can refute what I said!"

He has barely finished this remark when

Samek, who is on guard duty, signals to us to be silent. There is movement in the yard.

That night we give up our hot water. It is impossible to light the stove. The yard is teeming with soldiers.

It goes on like this for several days. I constantly ask myself what keeps us from going mad.

One thing alone makes life possible for us: we are beginning to believe that something important is about to happen outside. During the fourth night, at about five in the morning when it is nearly dawn, cannons start to thunder—but not in the usual way and not near us. Here in our neighborhood all is quiet. We can hear distant explosions. The artillery fire is so sustained and so violent that we hear it clearly, despite the distance. The cannons continue firing for hours and hours over a widespread area. Now we are certain an offensive has been launched somewhere.

We wait, hoping that the battle will come nearer. But nothing else happens. Here the silence continues.

Now it is almost eleven o'clock; the distant artillery fire grows fainter until it gradually ceases altogether. Disappointed, we lie down again. Isaac, who is on guard, rushes in and whispers that he can distinguish a massive troop movement coming from the Vistula. An aerial attack puts an end to our conversation. It is followed by several others.

One or another of us is constantly rushing to the entrance to try and make out what is happening up above. The troop movements have become spasmodic. We are unable to determine the direction these troops are taking. All that we are certain of is that something very important is taking place. We know that these are our last hours, indeed our last minutes, and that our fate depends upon the outcome of whatever it is that is happening over our heads.

Late in the night we clear the entrance and see great activity, now quite distant, not coming from Praga but from the opposite side. But it is happening too far away for us to make out clearly what it is all about.

Swiftly we block up the entrance again and keep silent. That important changes are taking place we do not doubt. But that things are moving so rapidly that the Germans, without fighting, have already evacuated the banks of the Vistula in the neighborhood of Praga . . . that is something we cannot even begin to imagine. And once more the cruel thought crosses our minds: Perhaps this time as well, it will all end up as it did before and we shall be doomed to stay in the bunker and perish there.

Weak in the extreme, we can scarcely stand up. This state of perpetual tension, this oscillation between hope and resignation, severely tests our already badly shaken nerves. The slightest thing can make us explode. Each of us broods in his corner. I can read the agitation on the faces of my companions. The silence is only interrupted by the moaning of Daniel, who is sick and in great pain. I go up to him and put my hand on his forehead: he has a raging fever. I smile at him, but at the same time my heart aches so much that I have to move away from him to hide my tears.

Wanting to control my emotion, I climb up to the entrance and look outside. The whiteness of the snow dazzles and at the same time refreshes me. From there I contemplate the bunker. I watch Hannah and Samek sitting so close to each other, looking into each other's eyes. I think to myself how beautiful it is to see two people so much in love. I imagine them a few days from now, lying just as they are now, near to each other, holding each other's hands in death. An overwhelming sense of pity suddenly takes hold of me. I forget that the same fate awaits me; perhaps my end is even closer than theirs. . . .

So I remain a long time, gazing into the darkness. I strain my ears in the hope of catching some noise which might reveal what is happening; but the silence enfolds me. Absolutely nothing can be heard.

This quiet begins to seem odd to me. I suddenly remember that usually after a day of hard fighting a few shots can still be heard during the night. They come from the sentries around about, firing into the air. Yet now even those shots are not heard. Why?

A thought rapidly crosses my mind, a mad thought, which sets my heart racing. Perhaps the Germans have already evacuated the area!

I go back down into the bunker. I outline the facts to everyone. I tell them about the things I have noticed. "It could be that we are already safe—that we are already free!"

My words arouse no reaction from them.

"We'll see about that tomorrow. Rest a little, Chaim."

That is all they find to say to me. I lie down in silence.

Next morning when day is well advanced, we do not hear any firing at all, only the throbbing of aircraft flying above us, very low, skirting the ground. Mechanically we sit up and wait for the usual noise of exploding bombs. But not a single bomb is dropped. And the planes are not even bothered by antiaircraft batteries.

I can wait no longer. I get up and climb to the exit. Isaac follows me. I remove one brick and then another. A bright light penetrates the bunker. I lean outside. Isaac is behind me. Cautiously we scale the mound of bricks covering our shelter and make our way down into the yard. We slip down into the streets, hugging the walls of ruined houses.

Around us everything seems to be dead. Off in the distance, on that same street, we see a child, a little girl of about eight. Near her is a woman bent down to the ground, busy clearing away the snow as though she is looking for something. We run toward them. As soon as she hears our footsteps, the woman gets up and, seeing us, quickly grabs the little girl by the hand.

"Who are you?" she asks, very frightened.

"We are Jews," I tell her. And I add immediately: "We've been hiding in a bunker; that's why we look this way."

"The Russians are here already—since yesterday!" she says.

"What?" I exclaim.

"Yes," the woman repeats. "Since yesterday. We are all free!"

I look at the child, then take her in my arms and kiss her.

We have no need to go back down into the bunker. Our cries of "We are free" have reached the ears of our comrades, who now come out into the street one by one. We fall into each other's arms and kiss one another. Hannah and Samek support Daniel, who is still very ill. Their faces are radiant with joy.

Kazik, our priest, crimson with emotion, shouts: "We've survived, we've survived!"

"Not all of us," Haskel murmurs, starting to stagger. Isaac holds him up and keeps him from collapsing.

Kazik puts his hand on Isaac's shoulder: "It will never happen again! Never! Never again!"

"Let us hope so," Isaac replies. Then he kisses him.

Ignace looks fixedly at a point on the horizon in the direction where his house once stood. He stands quite still. Tears flow down his cheeks. He murmurs: "My children, my children. . . ."

I look at the ruins all around us. All this wasteland that I once knew so well. Over there stand the ruins of the ghetto. And I think: The houses will be rebuilt, life will flourish here once again; but the Jews of Warsaw are no more.

In the distance we can hear soldiers singing as they march.

epilogue

Many years have passed since that day when seven Jews and a Polish priest came out of the darkness of a Warsaw bunker. But the bunker has left a lasting imprint on my way of thinking and feeling. Even today I am often transported in imagination beneath the ruins of the Warsaw Ghetto. Nightmares take me back to the bunker and the sewer. Again I struggle against the rats and freeze with terror at the sound of hobnailed boots.

Upon my return to France, I had the great happiness of finding my wife and two sons; that is why the memory of the bunker has not managed to cut me off from the world. But with each passing year, instead of fading from my mind, the memory became clearer. Finally, it drove me to take up my pen.

I wanted to put on record the part that Jews played in the 1944 insurrection in Warsaw. This has hardly been mentioned until now.

I wanted to express what I know about the attitude of the Polish people toward the Jew.

I have described what I saw with my own eyes and what I heard from my comrades in the bunker, without adding anything, without suppressing anything.

I am writing these words fifteen years after the experience in the bunker. As of this moment of writing, all of us who were part of that dark existence are still alive. Hannah married Samek;

they live in France. Isaac had the great good fortune to find his wife and child; they live in Australia. Daniel is reunited with one of his sisters in Belgium, where he has settled. Kazik lives in Poland and once more is a practicing priest. Haskel lives in Warsaw. Ignace lives in Israel.

My companions will certainly understand the emotion with which I have written this book, for even if there is in it only a faint echo of what we felt and suffered, yet on each page, with each description, I have lived through it all again.

To tell you the truth, all the time I have been writing this epilogue, I have felt myself plunged once more into the darkness of the bunker.

Charles Goldstein was born and raised in Poland. He emigrated to France in the 1920's and was active in the French Resistance during the Second World War. In June 1942 he was arrested by the Germans and sent to Auschwitz. In October 1943, he was sent together with other Jews to Warsaw, to clean up the ruins of the ghetto. *The Bunker* follows upon these events. Mr. Goldstein now makes his home in Paris, France.

Atheneum Paperbacks

TEMPLE BOOKS—*The Jewish Publication Society*

T1 JEWISH LIFE IN THE MIDDLE AGES *by Israel Abrahams*
T2 FOR THE SAKE OF HEAVEN *by Martin Buber*
T3 A HISTORY OF THE CONTEMPORARY JEWS *by Solomon Grayzel*
T4 THE ZIONIST IDEA *edited by Arthur Hertzberg*
T5 A HISTORY OF MEDIAEVAL JEWISH PHILOSOPHY *by Isaac Husik*
T6 THREE JEWISH PHILOSOPHERS *edited by Hans Lewy, Alexander Altmann and Isaak Heinemann*
T7 THE JEW IN THE MEDIEVAL WORLD *by Jacob R. Marcus*
T8 A HISTORY OF THE JEWISH PEOPLE *by Max L. Margolis and Alexander Marx*
T9 THE CONFLICT OF THE CHURCH AND THE SYNAGOGUE *by James Parkes*
T10 INTRODUCTION TO THE TALMUD AND MIDRASH *by Hermann L. Strack*
T11 AKIBA: SCHOLAR, SAINT AND MARTYR *by Louis Finkelstein*
T12 OF JEWISH LAW AND LORE *by Louis Ginzberg*
T13 JUDAISM AND MODERN MAN *by William Herberg*
T14 STUDIES IN JUDAISM *by Solomon Schechter*
T15 JEWISH MAGIC AND SUPERSTITION *by Joshua Trachtenberg*
T16 THE WILD GOATS OF EIN GEDI *by Herbert Weiner*
T17 JUDAISM AND CHRISTIANITY *by Leo Baeck*
T18 THEODORE HERZL *by Alex Bein*
T19 AMERICAN JEWRY AND THE CIVIL WAR *by Bertram W. Korn*
T20 SELECTED ESSAYS OF AHAD HA-'AM *by Leon Simon*
T21 NATIONALISM AND HISTORY *by Simon Dubnow*
T22 HELLENISTIC CIVILIZATION AND THE JEWS *by Victor Tcherikover*
T23 ANTHOLOGY OF HOLOCAUST LITERATURE *edited by Glatstein, Knox and Margoshes*
T24 FROM RESISTANCE TO DIPLOMACY *by Yehuda Bauer*
T25 JOSEPHUS *by Lion Feuchtwanger*
T26 BETWEEN EAST AND WEST *by André N. Choraqui*
T27 THE BUNKER *by Charles Goldstein*

PHILOSOPHY AND RELIGION

6 ROGER WILLIAMS *by Perry Miller*
9 MATTER, MIND AND MAN *by Edmund W. Sinnott*
19 BUDDHISM IN TRANSLATIONS *by Henry Clarke Warren*
31 PHILOSOPHY OF MATHEMATICS AND NATURAL SCIENCE *by Hermann Weyl*
38 TOWARD REUNION IN PHILOSOPHY *by Morton White*
52 RELIGION IN TWENTIETH CENTURY AMERICA *by Herbert W. Schneider*
60 HERACLITUS *by Philip Wheelwright*
69 ON THE USE OF PHILOSOPHY *by Jacques Maritain*
75 RELIGIOUS PHILOSOPHY *by Harry Austryn Wolfson*
97 THE EIGHTEENTH CENTURY CONFRONTS THE GODS *by Frank E. Manuel*
183 GENERALIZATION IN ETHICS *by Marcus Singer*
185 KARL MARX IN HIS EARLIER WRITINGS *by H. P. Adams*

Atheneum Paperbacks

LITERATURE AND THE ARTS

1 ROME AND A VILLA *by Eleanor Clark*
11 THE GRANDMOTHERS *by Glenway Wescott*
14 THE PRESENCE OF GRACE *by J. F. Powers*
18 THE SUDDEN VIEW *by Sybille Bedford*
25 THE ROBBER BRIDEGROOM *by Eudora Welty*
29 CONTEXTS OF CRITICISM *by Harry Levin*
36 GEORGE BERNARD SHAW *by Hesketh Pearson*
37 THE TERRITORY AHEAD *by Wright Morris*
39 THE LETTERS OF VINCENT VAN GOGH *edited by Mark Roskill*
42 THE GREEN MARE *by Marcel Aymé*
50 AMERICAN ARCHITECTURE AND OTHER WRITINGS *by Montgomery Schuyler, edited by William H. Jordy and Ralph Coe; abridged by William H. Jordy*
66 SELECTED POEMS INCLUDING THE WOMAN AT THE WASHINGTON ZOO *by Randall Jarrell*
76 THE SINGER OF TALES *by Albert B. Lord*
96 CONRAD THE NOVELIST *by Albert J. Guerard*
99 MARK TWAIN *by Henry Nash Smith*
102 EMILY DICKINSON *by Thomas H. Johnson*
112 THE LIFE OF THE DRAMA *by Eric Bentley*
114 SELECTED MARK TWAIN-HOWELLS LETTERS *edited by Frederick Anderson, William Gibson, and Henry Nash Smith*
122 REPORTING THE NEWS *edited by Louis M. Lyons*
131 WHAT IS THEATRE? *(incorporating* THE DRAMATIC EVENT*) by Eric Bentley*
135 THE HERO OF THE WAVERLY NOVELS *by Alexander Welsh*
143 POETS OF REALITY *by J. Hillis Miller*
158 LANGUAGE AND SILENCE *by George Steiner*
159 THE IMMEDIATE EXPERIENCE *by Robert Warshow*
165 MOVIES: A PSYCHOLOGICAL STUDY *by Martha Wolfenstein and Nathan Leites*
168 LITERARY DISSENT IN COMMUNIST CHINA *by Merle Goldman*
177 ALONE WITH AMERICA *by Richard Howard*
180 H. G. WELLS *by Lovat Dickson*
172 AMERICAN FICTION, 1920-1940 *by Joseph Warren Beach*
177 ALONE WITH AMERICA *by Richard Howard*
180 H. G. WELLS *by Lovat Dickson*
191 SNOW WHITE *by Donald Barthelme*
194 THE PRESENCE OF THE ACTOR *by Joseph Chaikin*

Atheneum Paperbacks

POLITICAL SCIENCE

2 POWER AND DIPLOMACY *by Dean Acheson*
15 CALL TO GREATNESS *by Adlai E. Stevenson*
20 DOCUMENTS ON FUNDAMENTAL HUMAN RIGHTS *edited by Zechariah*
A&B *Chafee, Jr., 2 vols.*
23 THE CONSTITUTION AND WHAT IT MEANS TODAY *by Edward S. Corwin*
27 COURTS ON TRIAL *by Jerome Frank*
34 THE DIPLOMACY OF ECONOMIC DEVELOPMENT *by Eugene R. Black*
40 THE UNITED STATES AND MEXICO *by Howard F. Cline*
41 THE DIPLOMATS, 1919-1939 *edited by Gordon A. Craig and Felix Gilbert,*
A&B *2 vols.*
44 CHINA'S RESPONSE TO THE WEST *by Ssu-Yü Teng and John K. Fairbank*
46 THE FUTURE OF FEDERALISM *by Nelson A. Rockefeller*
53 THE BILL OF RIGHTS *by Learned Hand*
54 STRATEGIC SURRENDER *by Paul Kecskemeti*
63 THE SINO-SOVIET CONFLICT, 1956-1961 *by Donald S. Zagoria*
72 MR. JUSTICE HOLMES AND THE SUPREME COURT *by Felix Frankfurter*
74 STALIN'S FOREIGN POLICY REAPPRAISED *by Marshall D. Shulman*
105 DILEMMAS OF URBAN AMERICA *by Robert C. Weaver*
107 RUSSIA LEAVES THE WAR *by George F. Kennan*
108 THE DECISION TO INTERVENE *by George F. Kennan*
110 DRED SCOTT'S CASE *by Vincent C. Hopkins, S.J.*
130 THE REVOLUTION OF THE SAINTS *by Michael Walzer*
138 OF LAW AND LIFE AND OTHER THINGS THAT MATTER *by Felix Frankfurter, edited by Philip B. Kurland*
147 AFTER IMPERALISM *by Akira Iriye*
148 POLITICAL CHANGE IN A WEST AFRICAN STATE *by Martin Kilson*
149 THE COMMUNIST CONTROVERSY IN WASHINGTON *by Earl Latham*
150 THE DECLINE OF AGRARIAN DEMOCRACY *by Grant McConnell*
156 VARIETIES OF POLICE BEHAVIOR *by James Q. Wilson*
157 AFRICA: FROM INDEPENDENCE TO TOMORROW *by David Hapgood*
160 UP AGAINST THE IVY WALL *by Jerry Avorn and other members of the staff of the* Columbia Daily Spectator
170 THE POLITICS OF AUTHENTICITY *by Marshall Berman*
175 SECOND CHANCE *by Robert A. Divine*
178 THE END OF THE AMERICAN ERA *by Andrew Hacker*
179 CONGRESS AND THE PUBLIC TRUST *by James C. Kirby, Jr.*
188 POLITICAL OBLIGATION *by Richard Flathman*
189 MACHIAVELLI AND THE NATURE OF POLITICAL THEORY *edited by Martin Fleisher*
195 MAN AND SOCIALISM IN CUBA *edited by Bertram Silverman*
196 THE RADICAL PROBE *by Michael W. Miles*
197 THE CRUEL CHOICE *by Denis Goulet*
198 POLITICS, LANGUAGE AND TIME *by J. G. A. Pocock*